FREUD AND THE HUMANITIES

FREUD AND THE HUMANITIES

edited by Peregrine Horden

ST. MARTIN'S PRESS
New York

 For information, write:
St. Martin's Press, Inc., 175 Fifth Avenue, New York, NY 10010
Printed in Great Britain

First published in the United States of America in 1985

ISBN 0-312-30542-7

Library of Congress Cataloging in Publication Data
Main entry under title:

Freud and the humanities.

Papers delivered at Oxford, All Souls College, 1984.
Bibliography: p.
Includes index.
Contents: Thoughts of Freud / Peregrine Horden — Symbolism, imagination, and biological destiny / Charles Rycroft — Psychoanalysis and creativity / Anthony Storr — [etc.]
1. Freud, Sigmund, 1856-1939—Influence—Addresses, essays, lectures. 2. Psychohistory—Addresses, essays, lectures. 3. Psychoanalysis and culture—Addresses, essays, lectures. I. Horden, Peregrine.

BF173.F85F725 1985 150.19'52 85-11940
ISBN 0-312-30542-7

Contents

Preface

The seven papers in this volume originate in the Chichele Lectures delivered in Oxford under the auspices of All Souls College during 1984.

The Lectures take their name from the College's founder, Henry Chichele, Archbishop of Canterbury from 1414 to 1443. Their history goes back to 1873, and to a proposal that the College invite 'distinguished foreigners or persons eminent in historical and literary inquiry' to deliver courses of lectures. The names suggested were those of the classical scholar Mommsen, three historians – Pauli, Ranke and Taine – Matthew Arnold and John Morley. The proposal did not at first commend itself, and it was only in 1909 that funds were set aside to support annual lectureships in 'foreign history' as a complement to the series of Ford's Lectures in English History. During the years 1912-1915 five Lecturers were appointed, including H.A.L. Fisher and Henri Pirenne. In 1925 the limitation to foreign history was removed, and since the revival of the Lectureship in 1946 the list of Lecturers has amply reflected the broad aims of the 1873 proposal. Lectures have been given by, among others, Arnold Toynbee, J. Dover Wilson, Edgar Wind, C.S. Lewis, Arthur Waley, Field Marshal Lord Montgomery, Lord Attlee, F.R. Leavis, Lord Robbins, Raymond Aron, Claude Shannon and Leszek Kolakowski. The 1982 series was the first in which each lecture was delivered by a different speaker (Alan Montefiore, Anthony Quinton, J.P. Stern, Jon Elster and Roger Scruton).

Lecturers have had the opportunity to revise their texts for publication, but the tone of the original occasion has been preserved throughout.

The editor is greatly indebted to the contributors for their patience and helpfulness in answering enquiries; and to Humaira Ahmed,

Simon Green, Paul Seabright, Alan Tyson and Judy Winchester for assistance in a variety of ways. Editorial faults remaining are my own.

All Souls College P.H.

Contributors

Peregrine Horden is a Fellow of All Souls College, Oxford.

Charles Rycroft is a practising psychotherapist and author of *The Innocence of Dreams* (1979).

Anthony Storr is Clinical Lecturer in Psychiatry and Fellow of Green College, Oxford. Among his books is *The Dynamics of Creation* (1972).

Richard Ellmann is Goldsmiths' Professor of English Literature in the University of Oxford. A revised edition of his biography of James Joyce was published in 1982.

Sir Ernst Gombrich is Emeritus Professor of the History of the Classical Tradition in the University of London. Among his volumes of essays is *Tributes: Interpreters of our Cultural Tradition* (1984).

S. Dresden is the retired Professor of Theory of Literature in the University of Leiden. His study of French Symbolism was published in 1981.

Francis Huxley is the author of *The Raven and the Writing-Desk* (1976) and *The Dragon* (1979).

Hugh Lloyd-Jones is Regius Professor of Greek and a Student of Christ Church, Oxford. A revised edition of his *The Justice of Zeus* was published in 1983.

Bibliographical note

Freud's writings are cited from *The Standard Edition of the Complete Psychological Works of Sigmund Freud*, translated under the general editorship of James Strachey in collaboration with Anna Freud, assisted by Alix Strachey and Alan Tyson, 24 vols (London, 1953-74), abbreviated as *SE*, by volume and page number. References in this form (e.g. *SE*, 5.21) can be 'translated' into references to the German *Studienausgabe* or *Gesammelte Werke* by recourse to Ingeborg Meyer-Palmedo, *Sigmund Freud-Konkordanz und -Gesamtbibliographie* (Frankfurt am Main, 1975).

With other writings, an English translation has been cited wherever possible.

Thoughts of Freud

Peregrine Horden

> I've always lived only in the *parterre* and basement of the building. You claim that with a change of viewpoint one is able to see an upper storey which houses such distinguished guests as religion, art, etc. You're not the only one who thinks that; most cultured specimens of *homo natura* believe it. In that you are conservative, I revolutionary. If I had another lifetime of work before me, I have no doubt that I could find room for these noble guests in my little subterranean house.
>
> Freud, letter to Ludwig Binswanger, 1936.[1]

> The monument of psychoanalysis must be traversed – not bypassed – like the fine thoroughfares of a very large city, across which we can play, dream, etc.: a fiction.
>
> Roland Barthes, *The Pleasure of the Text.*[2]

The extra lifetime's work denied to Freud has been granted to his adherents. Some of those noble guests can now find accommodation in the psychoanalytic basement – through developments which Freud could hardly have foreseen. New psychoanalytic methods of literary criticism in America provide one striking example of the devious and unexpected means by which his thought renews its claim to our attention. The history that explains these methods begins with Freud's early reputation outside Germany. Its middle chapters involve politics, philosophy and art as well as psychoanalysis. And it ends – for the moment – in this:

[1] Quoted by Ronald W. Clark, *Freud: The Man and the Cause* (London, 1982), p.497.
[2] London, 1976, p.58.

Thomas flang his sword into a bush.

It's not fair! he exclaimed.

What's not fair?

Why do I feel so bad? he asked, looking round him in every direction, as if for an answer.

Are you ill?

I could use a suck of the breast, Thomas said.

Not in front of him.

They retired from the Dead Father's view, behind a proliferation of Queen Anne's lace.

Donald Barthelme's novel *The Dead Father* obviously courts reference to the Oedipus complex.[3] It is indeed a product of the Freudian age – when the furtive ways of the unconscious are widely acknowledged, when the jargon of psychoanalysis has become a lingua franca, and when Freud's theories are an undisputed part of the novelist's potential subject matter.[4] Yet Barthelme's novel deliberately leaves us uncertain whether psychoanalysis is, as Barthes supposed, a plaything of the imagination or, as Freud hoped, a revolutionary and all-embracing means of interpretation. That uncertainty reflects its style. Like a French *nouveau roman* the novel is self-conscious about its fictionality. It systematically undermines the reader's habitual attempt to enter a credible imaginary world. Its heavy-handed allusions to Freud ironically 'resist' the analysis of either the author or his characters.

The psychoanalyst-critic is not to be outdone however. New perspectives await exploration. The narrative's inner workings, rather than the ostensible plot, become the focus of interest. The Dead Father of Barthelme's title is, we note, a giant, dead 'only in a sense'. He is being dragged towards his grave by lilliputian progeny. He lusts after his daughters in a manner reminiscent of Freud's discarded 'seduction theory'. But he is restrained by his otherwise ineffectual son, who learns how to cope from 'A Manual for Sons', reproduced as part of the text. Just as it ironically engages with traditional means of literary representation, so Barthelme's novel also confronts traditional literary images of the father. And this is more than a matter of surface allusion. It concerns the essence of the

[3] London, 1977. The quotation is from p.10.

[4] A point emphasized by Professor Ellmann in chapter 3.

novel as an example of discourse. Paternity is the clue to both structure and latent theme: to the very nature of the language being used.

> The death of fathers: When a father dies, his fatherhood is returned to the All-Father, who is the sum of all dead fathers taken together ... Fatherless now, you must deal with the memory of a father. Often that memory is more potent than the living presence of a father, is an inner voice commanding, haranguing, yes-ing and no-ing – a binary code, yes no yes no yes no yes no, governing your every, your slightest movement, mental or physical. At what point do you become yourself? Never, wholly, you are always partly him.[5]

That prompts a reading of the novel which Barthelme can anticipate but not forestall – in the psychoanalytic terms, less of Freud himself than of 'the French Freud', Jacques Lacan. It is not easy to give a brief account of ideas whose author prides himself on a style that imitates delirium. Suffice it to say that Lacan's radical psychoanalysis amounts to a rewriting of early Freud – *The Interpretation of Dreams*, *The Psychopathology of Everyday Life*, *Jokes and their Relation to the Unconscious* – in the light of post-structuralist theory of language. His analysis of infantile sexuality is couched in the vocabulary of signifier and signified that continental linguistics has learned from Saussure. The child's Oedipal encounter with the father marks its entry into 'the symbolic order' of culture, its constitution as a subject. A prior 'imaginary' mode of signification is exemplified by the child's unmediated desire to be what its mother desires (the 'phallus'): an inability, Lacan argues, to distinguish signifier from signified, word from object. This happy state gives way to the anxiety of post-structuralist discourse. In 'the symbolic order' words and objects never again coincide; the unity of the self is a precarious by-product of the yes-and-no of language.

> It is in the *name of the father* that we must recognize the support of the symbolic function which, from the dawn of history, has identified his person with the figure of the law.[6]

[5] *The Dead Father*, p.144.
[6] Lacan, *Ecrits: A Selection* (London, 1977), p.67.

The father's name, not the father himself. Only the signifier is ever present: the father himself is absent – dead 'in a sense', as Barthelme said. And desire has been pushed down into the unconscious, adding extra, concealed dimensions of meaning to the discourse which the name of the father initiates and authorizes. The unconscious, to quote Lacan's best-known utterance, is structured like a language. Its Freudian primary processes of condensation and displacement are reformulated in linguistic terms as metaphor and metonymy.

> There is in effect no signifying chain that does not have, as if attached to the punctuation of each of its units, a whole articulation of relevant contexts suspended 'vertically', as it were, from that point.[7]

The literary work can thus be anthropomorphized. The critic treats the text as an equivalent of unconscious discourse; he interprets the theme of the absent father as an allegory of the generation of covert meanings which repressed desire leaves beneath the surface. Lacan's analysis of Hamlet as being in 'a certain position of dependence upon the signifier' – that is, the phallus, of which Claudius is an incarnation – reveals the extent to which he has transformed Freudian theory.[8] The way is therefore open for a psychoanalytic approach not only to writers like Barthelme, but to Homer, Dickens or Faulkner as well, which seeks out the paternal signifier buried within the text.[9]

> The general action of the novel supposes that Esther's wise passivity, which establishes the positionality of the father in the new Bleak House, also casts back over the voice of the other who tells the public story of the reign of the symbolic order. Esther's narrative lays down the law of signification that permits this larger element of *Bleak House* to be given meaning.[10]

[7] *Ecrits*, p.154.

[8] Lacan, 'Desire and the interpretation of desire in Hamlet', *Yale French Studies*, 55-6 (1977), p.11. Cf. his 'Seminar on "The Purloined Letter" ', *Yale French Studies*, 48 (1972), a reading of Poe.

[9] Cf. *The Fictional Father: Lacanian Readings of the Text*, ed.Robert Con Davis (Amherst, Mass., 1981).

[10] Thomas A. Hanzo, 'Paternity and subject in *Bleak House*', *The Fictional Father*, p.43.

That there should be critical interpretation of Dickens guided by a structuralist version of French psychoanalysis and published in America in the 1980s is one of those paradoxes with which any appraisal of Freud's continuing impact must come to terms. What is striking is not the mixture of insight and absurdity which characterizes the enterprise: it is that psychoanalytic criticism of this sort should be practised in America at all.

America had, of course, welcomed psychoanalysis from the beginning. Freud rightly described the ideas he brought on his visit there of 1909 as 'the plague'. The environment had to some extent been prepared by, among others, Ernest Jones, James Jackson Putnam and William James, who cited the Freud-Breuer *Studies on Hysteria* with enthusiasm in his *The Varieties of Religious Experience.* The disease spread rapidly. But it was reduced to a state of mild endemicity by the 'neo-Freudians', who took their cue from the schismatic Alfred Adler. They elaborated an ego psychology which, in both theory and therapy, gave far more weight to the individual's socialization than to the instinctual origins of behaviour. Theirs was an optimistic, perhaps complacent, rereading of Freud which is still current.[11] Lacan, for whom there was no such thing as an autonomous ego or a reality principle, criticized them with unconcealed venom.[12] In literary circles meanwhile, the type of psychoanalytic interpretation whose major exponents included Edmund Wilson, Kenneth Burke and Lionel Trilling had lost its vitality by the 1960s. Their theories inevitably remained peripheral to a literary culture largely dominated by the New Criticism. Only Harold Bloom's idiosyncratic account of poetic influence as the 'belated' poet's Oedipal confrontation with his 'strong' predecessors testified thereafter to the continuing possibility of a respected Freudian criticism.[13]

So it is an alien form of literary exegesis that has come to be transplanted from France to America during the last twenty years. But the surprise is not only in the transplantation: that has to be seen in the wider intellectual context of the wholesale expropriation by

[11] Cf. J.A.C. Brown, *Freud and the Post-Freudians* (London, 1961); Russell Jacoby, *Social Amnesia: A Critique of Contemporary Psychology from Adler to Laing* (Boston, 1975).

[12] Cf. *Ecrits*, pp.6, 171.

[13] Cf. Bloom's *The Anxiety of Influence* (London, 1973), and *Poetry and Repression* (New Haven, 1976).

American universities, Yale especially, of post-structuralist theories associated with the name of Jacques Derrida.[14] What could not have been predicted twenty years ago was that there would be a French psychoanalysis worth adopting. Lacan's rise to preeminence – or notoriety – and the growth of a psychoanalytic culture around him owe a great deal, as Sherry Turkle has demonstrated, to the 'events' of 1968.[15] Lévi-Strauss's anthropology and structuralist linguistics had of course made their mark on French intellectual life well before then; and the schisms within the psychoanalytic establishment which would punctuate every stage of Lacan's career had already begun.[16] But until those decisive months of '68, combined hostility to Freud's thinking on the part of the Catholic Church, the Communist Party, the psychiatrists, the existentialists, and the prevailing 'bourgeois ideology', meant that there could be no such general enthusiasm for psychoanalysis in France as there had been in America. (Sartre's psychoanalytic biographies, of which Professor Ellmann speaks, represent the zeal of the late convert.)

In the land of Bergson and Janet psychoanalysis was looked on first as a German and then as an American inspiration – and thereafter to be distrusted. Freud's only real success with the French before the 1960s was among the Surrealists; and as Professor Dresden shows, it was a qualified success. That both Lacan and Lévi-Strauss should have frequented Surrealist circles in the early phase of their careers indicates the subsequent importance of this early link. Certainly, both were profoundly influenced by what they learned from the Surrealists. Lévi-Strauss has written in *Tristes tropiques* that psychoanalysis, Marxism and geology were what contributed most to his intellectual formation (each encouraging the search for structures hidden below the surface of things).[17] He has also, in true Surrealist fashion, said that his books write themselves. The obscurity of his style and mode of argument suggest that his anthropology has had more in common with both Surrealist writings and Lacan's delirious seminars (in which Surrealism was often

[14] Cf. Christopher Norris, *Deconstruction: Theory and Practice* (London, 1982), chapter 6, for a useful brief survey of the phenomenon.

[15] *Psychoanalytic Politics: Jacques Lacan and Freud's French Revolution* (London, 1979), to which I am generally indebted in what follows.

[16] Cf. Catherine Clément, *The Lives and Legends of Jacques Lacan* (New York, 1983).

[17] Harmondsworth, 1976, chapter 6.

mentioned) than differences of subject might lead us to suppose.[18] This community of interest would none the less have been insufficient by itself to shake the general antipathy to Freud's ideas.

1968 brought the catalyst of major change. Freud was no longer the preserve of Surrealists, their sympathizers, and a small number of analysts. Psychoanalytic slogans became rallying cries ('a policeman dwells in each of our heads, he must be killed'). The Sorbonne lecture hall, scene of protracted utopian debate, was rechristened *L'Amphithéâtre Che Guevara-Freud.* And like Marcuse, Reich and Foucault, Lacan was one of those elevated to the status which only the French seem capable of according their 'intellectuals'.[19] A new psychoanalytic ideology developed out of, and about, his ideas. In this ideology, the couch has become what the café was to the existentialists. Lacan's *Ecrits* is almost a coffee-table book, more venerated than read or understood. School children write essays on 'psychoanalysis and the notion of the epistemological break'. And *Freud Explained to Children* (with illustrations) is a popular gift.

Not only are there now more psychoanalysts than ever before in France; the very short sessions characteristic of Lacanians enable them to analyse more patients each day than is possible for an orthodox Freudian. The patients arrive expecting to talk about the name of the father and the like, some even clutching *Ecrits.* This vastly exacerbates the analyst's perennial problem of dealing with those who know too much for their own good, and who unconsciously create new forms of resistance out of psychoanalytic gleanings. And the outrageous, subversive quality of Lacan's thought is tamed into a set of nostrums much as Freud's own theories were domesticated by American ego psychology.

Renewed French interest in Freud (as mediated by Lacan) in the years around 1968 has, however, given rise to something more than another version of radical chic. A Lacanian approach to semiotics (the comparative investigation of signifiers) has resulted in textual exegesis more varied, and usually more subtle, than a search for symbolic fathers.[20] The rapprochement with Marxism prefigured in

[18] Transcripts of Lacan's *Séminaire* are being published in some twenty-four volumes.

[19] Régis Debray, '*Teachers, Writers, Celebrities: The Intellectuals of Modern France* (London, 1981), is the most recent analysis.

[20] Cf. Julia Kristeva, *Desire in Language* (Oxford, 1980), and Pierre Macherey's tentative use of Freud in *A Theory of Literary Production* (London, 1978).

the cult of Marcuse during '68 has gone beyond Marcuse's simplistic equation of psychic repression and political oppression – notably in some of Althusser's essays.[21] It has also led to *Anti-Oedipus*, the first instalment of a multi-volume work by Gilles Deleuze and Félix Guattari, designed to harmonize Freud with Marx once and for all, and to show the interdependence of Oedipal conflict and capitalism.[22]

The immense popularity of this work in France since its publication in 1972 is a further sign of how well Freud has been integrated into that bewildering blend of political rhetoric, linguistics and metaphysics which constitutes so much of modern French philosophy. In the early 1950s Merleau-Ponty, the leading phenomenologist, had all but rejected Freud's theory of the unconscious as having no bearing on the phenomenologist's method of philosophy by introspection. Just over a decade later Paul Ricoeur would, to the disgust of the Lacanians with whom he had been closely associated, publish a phenomenological 'close reading' of Freud (Freud only, not Lacan). He there asserted Freud's absolute centrality to the business of philosophical interpretation.[23] Echoing Ricoeur's 'situating' of Freud in contemporary debate, Vincent Descombes has summed up the change like this.

> In the recent evolution of philosophy in France we can trace the passage from the generation known after 1945 as that of the 'three H's' to the generation known since 1960 as that of the three 'masters of suspicion': the three H's being Hegel, Husserl and Heidegger, and the three masters of suspicion, Marx, Nietzsche and Freud.[24]

The usefulness of that triadic contrast perhaps leads Descombes to underestimate the extent to which Heidegger's thought has survived the period of transition. But his main point stands. Those continental schools of philosophy that lay as much emphasis on the material, especially the political, circumstances of a philosophical utterance as on its conceptual validity have naturally welcomed psychoanalysis to

[21] E.g. in *Lenin and Philosophy* (London, 1977).

[22] *Anti-Oedipus: Capitalism and Schizophrenia* (New York, 1977).

[23] *Freud and Philosophy: An Essay on Interpretation* (New Haven, 1977).

[24] *Modern French Philosophy* (Cambridge, 1980), p.3.

the philosophical ranks.[25] The common preoccupation of Nietzsche, Marx and Freud with the concealed origins and significance of human behaviour (in the will to power, in material interest or in libido) is immediately relevant to a post-structuralist concern with the elusiveness of meaning. That is why, for example, Freud's work is frequently referred to by Derrida, currently the most widely-known and controversial of French philosophers. Freud, like Lacan, and indeed like many others, may be the victim of Derrida's deconstructive exegesis. Yet his thought is also exemplary for the philosophical exposure of the 'metaphysics of presence' which Derrida finds in western thought.

> That the present in general is not primal but, rather, reconstituted, that it is not the absolute, wholly living form which constitutes experience, that there is no purity of the living present – such is the theme, formidable for metaphysics, which Freud, in a conceptual scheme unequal to the thing itself, would have us pursue. This pursuit is doubtless the only one which is exhausted neither within metaphysics nor within science.[26]

* * *

In 1914, already reflecting on the history of the psychoanalytic movement, Freud predicted that 'the scene of the decisive struggle over psycho-analysis' would be the ancient centres of culture where the greatest resistance to his ideas had been displayed.[27] Even so, he might have been startled to learn of his current popularity and intellectual standing in France – and of his appeal, through Lacan, to novelists and literary critics in America, for so long the land of ego psychology. Yet he would not have been surprised to find himself dubbed a master of suspicion, a Derridean – to use a phrase ripe for deconstruction – *avant la lettre*.[28]

The mastery was evinced, and the ultimate reputation for it assured, by a relatively small body of work. Had Freud published

[25] Cf. *Philosophy in France Today*, ed. Alan Montefiore (Cambridge, 1983), especially the editor's Introduction.

[26] Derrida, 'Freud and the scene of writing', in *Writing and Difference* (London, 1978), p.212. Derrida also 'reads' Freud – and Lacan – in *La carte postale* (Paris, 1980).

[27] *SE*, 14.32.

[28] Cf. Samuel Weber, *The Legend of Freud* (Minneapolis, 1982).

only *The Interpretation of Dreams*, the *Three Essays on the Theory of Sexuality* and various supporting papers, he would have given Lacan and Derrida quite enough material with which to refashion him in their own image. His contribution to modern thought would hardly have been diminished. And others could have proceeded to extend his systematic impieties (as Kenneth Burke once described them) beyond the realm of individual psychology with ample theoretical justification.

Indeed, one possible view of Freud seeks to protect him from his own and his disciples' extravagances. It sees his clinical work as the essence of his achievement: that communion of one unconscious with another which constitutes the analysis of the neurotic. It has little time for the wanton speculation about the unconscious significance of cultural phenomena that was characteristic of the first generation of pupils, such as Rank or Ferenczi (for whom all containers were womb-like and all swords penial). And it reminds us that Freud's ventures of this kind, whether on Leonardo or Moses, literature or society, were often tentatively conceived, reluctantly published, and readily disavowed. (As Freud said to Abram Kardiner of *Totem and Taboo*, 'don't take that seriously – I made that up on a rainy Sunday afternoon'.)[29]

Not only have such diversions been extraordinarily influential; they actually lie at the very heart of Freud's thinking – whatever he may have said about them. They are as central to the psychoanalytic project as clinical observation; and they followed ineluctably from what Freud was observing and thinking. It was he, not Jung or any of the other early followers, who liberated psychoanalysis from the regime of consultancy. The omnicompetence he claimed for his technique of explanation was inherent in the nature of psychoanalysis as a general theory of the mind and as the science of the unconscious.

Historically, the point is easily documented. There are no wholly separate periods in Freud's work, apart from his long pre-psychoanalytic involvement with neurophysiology (and historians are now beginning to see even that as deeply pertinent to the genesis of his

[29] Quoted by Clark, *Freud*, p.355. Cf. Bruno Bettelheim, *Freud and Man's Soul* (New York, 1983), for the argument that Freud aimed at individual self-knowledge, not general science.

most significant ideas).[30] There was, admittedly, in the 1920s a return to the psychology of the ego, a subject which Freud can be seen to have neglected since the (posthumously published) *Project for a Scientific Psychology* of 1895. And Freud himself wrote in his *Autobiographical Study* that his scientific career had been a long detour away from his original interest in problems of human culture – to which, newly-armed with the theory of the death instinct from *Beyond the Pleasure Principle*, he returned at the end of the '20s in *The Future of an Illusion* and *Civilization and its Discontents*.

But these are shifts of emphasis, not fresh departures. As the lists of Freud's writings by subject matter included in the Standard Edition reveal at a glance, the psychoanalysis of the arts and of anthropological topics like myth and religion interested him from the beginning.[31] The behaviour of 'savage tribes in antiquity' was first discussed, not in *Totem and Taboo* but (albeit briefly) in a pre-psychoanalytic essay on hysterical paralysis which Freud probably began to write in 1886.[32] The reflections on the Oedipus complex in Sophocles and Shakespeare in *The Interpretation of Dreams*[33] are, like so many other aspects of Freud's thought, fully anticipated in a letter to Wilhelm Fliess of the late 1890s written during Freud's self-analysis. And it is notable that he should immediately turn for confirmation of a very personal discovery to works of literature.

> One single thought of general value has been revealed to me. I have found, in my own case too, falling in love with the mother and jealousy of the father, and I now regard it as a universal event of early childhood, even if not so early as in children who have been made hysterical … If that is so, we can understand the riveting power of *Oedipus Rex*, in spite of all the objections raised by reason against its presupposition of destiny … A fleeting idea has passed through my head of whether the same thing may not lie at the bottom of *Hamlet* as well.[34]

[30] Cf. Frank J. Sulloway, *Freud: Biologist of the Mind* (London, 1979), the most controversial of the revisionists.

[31] *SE*, 13.162 (anthropology, mythology, religion); 21.213-14 (art, literature, aesthetics).

[32] *SE*, 1.170.

[33] *SE*, 4.261f.

[34] 15 October 1897, *SE*, 1.265.

With Freud, fleeting ideas had a habit of becoming certainties. The creative élan with which he at once turned his hand to the interpretation of whatever facet of social life engaged him is amply demonstrated in other letters to Fliess:

> ... The idea of bringing in the witches is gaining strength, and I think it hits the mark. Details are beginning to crowd in. Their 'flying' is explained; the broomstick they ride on is probably the great Lord Penis. Their secret gatherings, with dancing and other amusements, can be seen any day in the streets where children play ... The story of the Devil, the vocabulary of popular swear-words, the songs and habits of the nursery – all these are now gaining significance for me ... In connection with the dancing in witches' confessions, remember the dance-epidemics in the Middle Ages ... I have an idea shaping in my mind that in the perversions, of which hysteria is the negative, we may have before us a residue of a primaeval sexual cult which, in the Semitic East (Moloch, Astarte), was once more, perhaps still is, a religion ...[35]

Art, history, folklore, anthropology, comparative religion: Freud's vast reading supplied material in abundance.[36] Psychoanalysis was not first evolved and then applied. Its application contributed greatly to its evolution. For this reason, and also because of the paucity of case-histories with which they were familiar, Freud's disciples who met regularly – and under his strict personal supervision – at the Vienna Psychoanalytical Society ranged as widely as he did during the movement's early years.[37] Their first three recorded meetings, in October 1906, were taken up with Otto Rank's distillation of the incest motif from poetry and folklore. During the course of these, in interesting contrast to Professor Gombrich's exposition, father hatred was identified as a dominant motif in Schiller's work. And Freud opined that incest was rare in Shakespeare because he adapted existing plots and his texts were therefore 'not really his own'. Those

[35] 24 January 1897, *SE*, 1.242-3. Cf. 17 January, 1.242, on hysteria and the medieval theory of possession.

[36] Freud's learning, and the scope of the comparisons he was always drawing in order to clarify his arguments, are well brought out by Peter Gay in *Freud, Jews and Other Germans* (Oxford, 1979), and by the 'List of analogies' in *SE*, 24.179f.

[37] *Minutes of the Vienna Psychoanalytical Society*, ed. Herman Nunberg and Ernst Federn, 3 vols (New York, 1962-74).

later subjected to analysis included Christ, Oedipus, Goethe, Kleist, Hoffmann and Dostoevsky. There was also talk of the 'psychic life of the nation', primitive agriculture, and 'the corset in custom and usage among the peoples of the world'.

The group's catholicity was to be echoed in the journal *Imago*, published between 1912 and 1941 and devoted to the non-medical applications of psychoanalysis. In its first issue Freud stressed the need to extend the scope of psychoanalysis to subjects as diverse as criminology, philology and ethics, as well as myth and religion. And in later years the journal included, among numerous other works from his pen, the essays ultimately collected as *Totem and Taboo* and *Moses and Monotheism*.

No one, indeed, was more catholic in analytical research than Freud. The economy and subtlety of his arguments are always betrayed by rapid summaries, which make them sound like the caricatures of interpretation to which Freud's disciples were generally so prone. But certain recurrent themes do emerge. Setting aside an interest in occultism (which Freud had in common with Jung to a greater extent than is often realized)[38] and in the use of analysis in legal proceedings,[39] there are five main themes in what might be summed up as his psychoanalysis of culture.[40]

One theme comprises Freud's successive polemical accounts of the instinctual elements in contemporary religious belief and practice. Early on, he drew a celebrated analogy between religious observance and obsessional neurosis.[41] In his book on Leonardo God appeared as 'the exalted father'; he explained the cohesion of the Catholic Church in libidinal terms in *Group Psychology and the Analysis of the Ego*; trust in God was a substitute for paternal protection in *The Future of an Illusion*; religious sentiment was 'oceanic' – involving regression to a primitive stage of ego development – in *Civilization and its Discontents*.

[38] Cf. Ernest Jones, *Sigmund Freud: Life and Work* (London, 1953-7), 3.402f., a tactful summary; *SE*, 18.176.

[39] *SE*, 9.

[40] No attempt is made in what follows to give a proper digest of Freud's theories. It will be enough to refer to the best short account: Richard Wollheim, *Freud*, Modern Masters (London, 1971); and to the best long account: Philip Rieff, *Freud: The Mind of the Moralist*, 3rd edition (Chicago and London, 1979). The most intelligent, and intelligible, philosophical exploration is that by Paul Ricoeur, *Freud and Philosophy*.

[41] *SE*, 9.

A second theme, bound up in this analysis of religion as the 'neurotic' product of instinctual renunciation, is the interpretation of culture (or civilization) as ever-stronger repression – with the probability of corporate neurosis, rather than sublimation, increasing in proportion. 'We may well raise the question whether our "civilized" sexual morality is worth the sacrifice which it imposes on us,' Freud wrote in 1908.[42] And by the time of *Civilization and its Discontents* (1930) the conflict at the heart of culture had been rendered still more insoluble (and indeed confused in its theoretical presentation) by the inclusion of the death instinct. For in Freud's early formulations, civilization was a sacrifice of libidinal instinct for the sake of ego instinct, or self-preservation. But now:

> civilization is a process in the service of Eros, whose purpose is to combine single human individuals, and after that families, then races, peoples and nations, into one great unity, the unity of mankind. Why this has to happen, we do not know; the work of Eros is precisely this. These collections of men are to be libidinally bound to one another. Necessity alone, the advantages of work in common, will not hold them together. But man's natural aggressive instinct, the hostility of each against all and of all against each, opposes this programme of civilization. This aggressive instinct is the derivative and the main representative of the death instinct which we have found alongside of Eros and which shares world-dominion with it. And now, I think, the meaning of the evolution of civilization is no longer obscure to us. It must present the struggle between Eros and Death, between the instinct of life and the instinct of destruction, as it works itself out in the human species.[43]

We have to interpret the subjects of Freud's biographical interest, the third theme in his writings, as figures in this dire secular drama. The most distinguished 'pathographies' are those of the creative artists whose works may be used to shed light on their neuroses (the book's title is, after all, *Leonardo da Vinci and a Memory of his Childhood*). But, despite differences in the evidence used, no significant distinction should be drawn between Freud's studies of Leonardo, Jensen, Goethe and Dostoevsky and his analyses of Woodrow

[42] *SE*, 9.204.
[43] *SE*, 21.122.

Wilson or Dr Schreber.

The fourth theme in his work is the comparative analysis of material whose underlying similarity Freud had already asserted in letters to Fliess, where he set the Sophocles play alongside his own Oedipal memories and the history of witchcraft alongside children's games and symptoms of hysteria. It all began with *The Interpretation of Dreams*. 'Previously,' Freud later explained,

> psycho-analysis had only been concerned with solving pathological phenomena ... But when it came to dreams, it was no longer dealing with a pathological symptom, but with a phenomenon of normal mental life which might occur in any healthy person. If dreams turned out to be constructed like symptoms, if their explanation required the same assumptions – the repression of impulses, substitutive formation, compromise-formation, the dividing of the conscious and the unconscious into various psychical systems – then psycho-analysis was no longer an auxiliary science in the field of psychopathology, it was rather the starting-point of a new and deeper science of the mind which would be equally indispensable for the understanding of the normal.[44]

This discovery is, for example, what underlies Freud's interest in the similarity between the purported antithetical meanings of words in ancient languages and the double meaning of certain elements in dreams; or his analysis of 'the theme of the three caskets' in myth, lore and Shakespearian drama; or his ethnography of the virginity taboo.[45]

It also, of course, underlies that amalgam of anthropology, history and theory of the neuroses that constitutes *Totem and Taboo*. But this work, together with its sequel on Moses, is best seen as representative of the fifth and last of the preoccupations which inform Freud's non-clinical writings: a search for origins. 'Another presentiment ... tells me, as I knew already – though in fact I know nothing at all,' Freud had written to Fliess in May 1897, 'that I shall very soon discover the source of morality ...'[46] In *Totem and Taboo* Freud triumphantly located the source not only of morality, but of

[44] *SE*, 20.47.
[45] *SE*, 11, 12.
[46] *SE*, 1.253.

religion, society and the incest taboo, in the aftermath of the aboriginal patricide. The book on Moses revealed the origins of monotheistic religion in the murder which re-enacted that of the primal father. And Freud elsewhere had a miscellany of like speculations to offer: on the acquisition of fire for example (a renunciation of homosexual erotism), and on the origins of clothing (women, inspired by pubic hair, invented weaving to conceal their lack of a penis).[47]

These last two features of the evolution of Freud's thought – the comparative study of symptoms, dreams and myths, and the search for prehistoric origins – are both crucial to the psychoanalysis of culture. The broadening of explanatory scope from the aetiology of the neuroses to the origins of weaving depended upon a series of increasingly bold theoretical steps. The first was to generalize from the pathological to the normal in human affairs. The second was to dispense with the 'patient's' free associations and thus to make possible a historical and sociological psychoanalysis.[48] The third was to postulate that the interpretation of works of art, myths, folklore and primitive behaviour could all be interpreted in the same way as dreams, jokes, slips and symptoms; for all of them originated in universal 'archaic' processes of the mind such as condensation, displacement and symbolization.[49]

The argument supporting this postulate was, at heart, circular. Freud had used Sophocles's *Oedipus* to give shape and substance to the results of his self-analysis; but he then sought to demonstrate the play's latent content by referring to its universal power of awakening unconscious memories such as his own.[50] A further step was necessary: the extension from biology to psychology of Haeckel's biogenetic law.[51] If ontogeny recapitulates phylogeny, if the stages of individual development reflect those of mankind, then primitive man

[47] *SE*, 22.187f., 132.

[48] Cf. *SE*, 4.241, and Rieff, *Freud*, p.103.

[49] It would be of interest to explore the similarities between Freud's view of primitive mentality and that of his contemporary, the sociologist Lucien Lévy-Bruhl (1857-1939), whose work Freud apparently did not know. Cf. Lévy-Bruhl's *Les fonctions mentales dans les sociétés inférieures* (Paris, 1910).

[50] Cf. Ricoeur, 'Freud and the work of art', in *Psychiatry and the Humanities*, vol. 1, ed. Joseph H. Smith (New Haven and London, 1976).

[51] Cf. Stephen Jay Gould, *Ontogeny and Phylogeny* (Cambridge, Mass., and London, 1977).

the myth-maker was genuinely childlike in psychological make-up. The final step – conceptually not chronologically – in this methodological progression was to adopt the Lamarckian theory that acquired characteristics could be genetically inherited.

Freud's unswerving adherence to Lamarck's discredited theory (which he at one stage planned to reformulate in psychoanalytic terms)[52] has often been considered a minor aberration confined to the books on totemism and Moses and having no bearing on the rest of his achievement. Certainly, the most obvious use of the theory was in the explanation of a sense of guilt in monotheistic religion as a genetically inherited memory trace of murdering the primal father. But Freud invoked it on numerous occasions, calling its incorporation into his ideas 'the coping-stone of psychoanalysis';[53] and it may also have coloured his hypotheses about infant sexuality.[54] Like so much else, Lamarckianism is prefigured in the Fliess correspondence, where Freud speculates on the hereditary transmission of acquired neuroses.[55] Its full deployment seems, however, to have been precipitated by his analysis of the 'Wolf Man', from which he could confirm the universality of the Oedipus complex as a 'hereditary schema' independent of individual experience.[56] And in the twenty-third *Introductory Lecture*, during a discussion of infantile fantasy, Freud had this to say:

> The only impression we gain is that these events of childhood are somehow demanded as a necessity, that they are among the essential elements of a neurosis. If they have occurred in reality, so much to the good; but if they have been withheld by reality, they are put together from hints and supplemented by phantasy. The outcome is the same, and up to the present we have not succeeded in pointing to any difference in the consequences, whether phantasy or reality has had the greater share in these events of childhood. Here we simply have once again one of the complemental relations that I have so often

[52] Jones, *Freud*, 3.330f.

[53] *A Psycho-Analytic Dialogue: The Letters of Sigmund Freud and Karl Abraham 1907-1926*, ed. Hilda C. Abraham and Ernst L. Freud (London, 1965), pp.261-2.

[54] The most extreme interpretation of Freud as a Lamarckian is that of Sulloway, *Freud: Biologist of the Mind*, who misinterprets some texts to suit his theory.

[55] *SE*, 1.184; *The Origins of Psycho-Analysis*, ed. Marie Bonaparte, Anna Freud and Ernst Kris (London, 1954), p.72 – a letter not included in *SE*, 1.

[56] *SE*, 17.119.

> mentioned; moreover it is the strangest of all we have met with. Whence comes the need for these phantasies and the material for them? There can be no doubt that their sources lie in the instincts; but it has still to be explained why the same phantasies with the same content are created on every occasion. I am prepared with an answer which I know will seem daring to you ... It seems to me quite possible that all things that are told to us to-day in analysis as phantasy ... were once real occurrences in the primaeval times of the human family, and that children in their phantasies are simply filling in the gaps in individual truth with prehistoric truth. I have repeatedly been led to suspect that the psychology of the neuroses has stored up in it more of the antiquities of human development than any other source.[57]

Lamarckianism was not peripheral to his thought: it was absolutely central. 'The psychological peculiarities of families, races and nations, even in their attitude to analysis, allow of no other explanation.'[58]

Realizing the strength and pervasiveness of this conviction is more than a scholarly matter of accurate biography. It helps us judge between two possible versions of Freud – and we can therefore estimate whether the psychoanalysis of culture that others have performed in his name is a travesty or a continuation of what he set out to achieve.

Throughout his career Freud wavered in answering the questions that must constantly be rehearsed by those who grant psychoanalysis any credence at all. How much can psychoanalysis interpret and explain? At what point in human affairs do conscious and preconscious motives yield to unconscious ones? After hearing a paper on chess at a meeting of his infant Psychoanalytical Society Freud remarked: 'this is the kind of paper that will bring psychoanalysis into disrepute. You cannot reduce everything to the Oedipus complex. Stop!'[59] There is the first of the two Freuds speaking. For him, psychoanalysis was the science of the unconscious; it had as little to say about the 'normal' psychology of

[57] *SE*, 16.370-1.
[58] *SE*, 23.240. Cf. *SE*, 7.225, 13.188, 19.37-8, 23.101; Sulloway, chapter 10.
[59] Reported by Abram Kardiner. Quoted by Clark, *Freud*, p.216. Cf. *SE*, 17.72, 21.171.

everyday life, the ego's encounter with the cultural environment, as chemistry had to say about biology.[60] 'Starting from unconscious perception,' he wrote in *An Outline of Psycho-Analysis*, his final summation, the ego

> has subjected to its influence ever larger regions and deeper strata of the id, and, in the persistence with which it maintains its dependence on the external world, it bears the indelible stamp of its origin (as it might be 'Made in Germany').[61]

Such was socialization – a process to be noted, not explained; but a process which was none the less of enormous significance for psychoanalysis. Freud always held that the possible aetiologies of neuroses should be seen as a 'complemental series' of endogenous and exogenous factors, with the two extremes of the spectrum of possible combinations seldom occurring.[62] Symptoms were, in his terminology, 'compromise formations' between unconscious and preconscious, caused by instinct but shaped by external circumstance.[63] Myths were, similarly, the distorted secular dreams of youthful humanity.[64] The unconscious meaning of works of art could be more or less obscure according to what sort of tradition nourished the 'individual talent' and how advanced (in terms of repression) was the culture which sustained the tradition; the Oedipal content of *Hamlet* was thus better hidden than that in Sophocles's play, as the Elizabethans were generally more neurotic than the Greeks.[65]

There is, then, according to this view of Freud, a great deal of 'normal' life in which psychoanalysis should take no interest. (Even Lacan seems to have recognized that.)[66] And there are a great many phenomena of which it can never produce a sufficient explanation. The similarity between diabolical possession and hysteria which Freud – and Charcot before him – had already noticed in the

[60] *SE*, 18.252.
[61] *SE*, 23.199. 'Made in Germany' is in English in the original.
[62] Cf. *SE*, 3.135-6, and the twenty-second and twenty-third *Introductory Lectures*.
[63] Cf. *SE*, 14.53, 126.
[64] *SE*, 9.152.
[65] Cf. Ricoeur, 'Psychoanalysis and the work of art'.
[66] *Ecrits*, p.163.

1880s[67] could, for example, no more lead to a full historical account of possession than obsessional neurosis could be a complete explanation of a particular religious observance. 'We need not be surprised to find,' Freud wrote in 'A seventeenth-century demonological neurosis' of 1923,

> that, whereas the neuroses of our unpsychological modern days take on a hypochondriacal aspect and appear disguised as organic illnesses, the neuroses of those early times appear in demonological trappings ... The states of possession correspond to our neurosis ... In our eyes, the demons are bad and reprehensible wishes, derivatives of instinctual impulses that have been repudiated and repressed. We merely eliminate the projection of these mental entities into the external world which the middle ages carried out.[68]

Why such projections took one form rather than another is a question for history rather than for psychoanalysis. And the analogy of religion and neurosis turns out, on similar grounds, to be no more than that – an analogy.[69]

Freud's aesthetics can, after the same fashion, be interpreted as both circumspect and incomplete. We may take seriously his frequent disclaimers that psychoanalysis by itself provides a full understanding of a work of art's origins. As several of the discussions that follow emphasize, psychoanalysis really has nothing to say about the nature of artistic talent. (This is perhaps because Freud's theory of art did not keep pace with his developing views on the constructive power of the unconscious.)[70] It could be added that Freud adhered to an impoverished quasi-Aristotelian conception of aesthetic response; that he only dealt with artistic form as a 'fore-pleasure' which bribes the spectator to pay attention; and that he had little to say about how sublimation occurs.[71] Freud as the tentative

[67] *SE*, 1.242 (Letter 56 to Fliess); Cf. 3.20.

[68] *SE*, 19.72. Cf. 11.50, 13.64-5.

[69] Cf. *SE*, 21.43-4.

[70] See Richard Wollheim, *On Art and the Mind* (London, 1973), p.219. 'Dostoevsky and parricide' (1928), *SE*, 21, was Freud's only substantial essay on art after *Leonardo da Vinci* (1910).

[71] Cf. Ricoeur, 'Psychoanalysis and the work of art', and *Freud and Philosophy*, pp.163f. Attempts have been made to extrapolate from Freud's theory of jokes to a general psychoanalysis of art. Cf. E.H. Gombrich, 'Verbal wit as a paradigm of art', in his *Tributes* (Oxford, 1984); Jack J. Spector, *The Aesthetics of Freud* (London, 1972).

aesthetician is perhaps encapsulated by reference, not to the Leonardo essay but to Rembrandt. Freud told Jones that Rembrandt was his favourite painter.[72] And the series of self-portraits is surely the greatest psychological document in the history of art. Yet Freud recognized its opacity to an analysis like those he offered of *Gradiva* or 'Moses'. He left the series alone.

The modest Freud had a more ambitious internal counterpart. It was the other Freud, who, in his eightieth year, pronounced the agenda for psychoanalysis used here as an epigraph. This is the man in whose eyes 'the whole course of the history of civilization *is no more than* an account of the various methods adopted by mankind for "binding" their unsatisfied wishes'.[73] The reduction was made possible by postulating that the 'myth-work' and the 'art-work' (to invent Freudian terminology) were on the same spectrum of disguised wish-fulfilments as the joke-work and the dream-work. And Haeckel and Lamarck were enlisted so that what escaped analysis on the purely synchronic front could be caught by analysis on the historical front, and then restored to the contemporary picture as an inherited repression. Form and content, tradition and individual talent, symptom and neurosis: nothing escaped.

> A child who produces instinctual repressions spontaneously is thus merely repeating a part of the history of civilization. What is to-day an act of internal restraint was once an external one, imposed, perhaps, by the necessities of the moment; and, in the same way, what is now brought to bear upon every growing individual as an external demand of civilization may some day become an internal disposition to repression.[74]

All that psychoanalysis needed was patience.

* * *

'Thoughts of Freud, naturally.'[75] Such was Franz Kafka's reaction on reading over one of his own stories the night after he had finished writing it. Kafka has been called the Dante of the post-Freudian age.

[72] Jones, *Freud*, 3.441. Cf. *SE*, 6.227-8.

[73] *SE*, 13.186, my italics.

[74] *SE*, 13.188-9.

[75] Quoted by Walter H. Sokel, 'Freud and the magic of Kafka's writing', in *The World of Franz Kafka*, ed. J.P. Stern (London, 1980), p.146.

But what that age thinks of Freud – what it has made of his manifold legacy – defies even supremely creative epitomizing. The contributors to this volume had a less demanding brief: to discover what thoughts of Freud occur in surveying some aspect of those variously defined fields of endeavour, the study of the arts and – what on many definitions subsumes it – the humanities. The collection thus encompasses poetry but not politics, anthropology but not experimental psychology. And this obedience to rough and ready definitions also accords with Freud's lifelong enthusiasms. The subjects involved are, indeed, those about which he had a good deal to say and on which his thinking has imposed itself most forcibly. The exact scope, emphasis and tone of each contribution varies with the promptings of its chosen area – between Freud's own ideas and those of disciples, dissidents and later admirers; between the history of his influence and the criticism of what has resulted from it. The historical portion spans the one movement which has been most receptive to psychoanalysis (Surrealism) and the discipline which has perhaps ultimately proved most recalcitrant (social anthropology). The criticism ranges from severity to guarded approbation.

This independence of both approach and conclusion is essential. The problem of determining what is to count as influence can hardly be solved *a priori* – something which literary criticism has apparently conceded in replacing 'influence' with 'intertextuality' or 'discourse' as an all-purpose linking term less redolent of personal encounter. Tracing Freud's impact on the humanities is not only a search for ideological paternity – who read whom – in all its Oedipal horror. It is also, more importantly, like Freud's own work an archaeology: the uncovering of obscure paradigms of thought. The seven essays collected here form part of a far larger enterprise that, despite the volume of commentary psychoanalysis has engendered, is only now beginning in scholarly and critical earnest.

Additional assessments could therefore have been included: of the rise and fall of psychohistory for example, from Freud's *Leonardo* to the psychogenetic theory of everything propounded by Lloyd deMause;[76] of the unexpected fortunes of Freud in the field of art

[76] See *The History of Childhood: The Evolution of Parent-Child Relationships as a Factor in History*, ed. Lloyd deMause (New York, 1974). Cf. David E. Stannard, *Shrinking History: On Freud and the Failure of Psychohistory* (New York and Oxford, 1980).

history, typified in the application of Kleinian theory to architectural criticism by Adrian Stokes;[77] of psychoanalysis in sociology, from Talcott Parsons to the Frankfurt School of Marxists, or in Anglo-American philosophy from Wittgenstein to Davidson.[78] There is always more to be said. And this is not merely because each age and culture reinterprets orthodox psychoanalysis to suit its own purposes; it is mainly because, as Dr Rycroft observes, psychoanalysis itself is being continually reformulated. The American 'psychoanalytic psychologist of the self' Heinz Kohut has for instance, like Freud and Lacan, held forth on Shakespeare, as well as on that most Freudian of modern writers, Thomas Mann. A new set of doctrines provides a new analysis of culture.[79]

Just as there is more to be said of Freud and his epigones so there is more to be uncovered about those on whom they have depended. Two problems arise. The first is that to which Professor Lloyd-Jones adverts: of Freud's own ambiguous place in the history of ideas. A good writer, Nietzsche proposed in *Human, All-Too Human*, has not only his own mind but the minds of his friends as well. It is only since the publication of Ellenberger's massive work *The Discovery of the Unconscious* that we have grown used to disregarding the legend of Freud as an isolated hero battling for recognition in a hostile scientific environment.[80] Increasingly, the early development of psychoanalysis comes to seem like a creative synthesis of numerous existing scientific ideas – each of which may well have been as influential on modern culture as psychoanalysis itself. We must beware of attributing too much to Freud – or at least to Freud alone. And that caution should lead to an adequate recognition of the writers of all kinds whose thought psychoanalysis has embraced or unwittingly echoed. In a characteristic early essay Auden remarked

[77] Cf. Spector, *The Aesthetics of Freud*, chapter 4. On Stokes see Roger Scruton, *The Aesthetics of Architecture* (London, 1979), chapter 6, and Wollheim, *On Art and the Mind*, chapter 15.

[78] Cf. Yannis Gabriel, *Freud and Society* (London, 1983); *Philosophical Essays on Freud*, ed. Richard Wollheim and James Hopkins (Cambridge, 1982).

[79] On Kohut see Ernest S. Wolf, 'Psychoanalytic psychology of the self and literature', *New Literary History*, 12 (1980).

[80] Henri F. Ellenberger, *The Discovery of the Unconscious: The History and Evolution of Dynamic Psychiatry* (London, 1970), especially pp.534f. Cf. Sulloway, *Freud: Biologist of the Mind*, and Hannah S. Decker, *Freud in Germany: Revolution and Reaction in Science, 1893-1907* (New York, 1977).

that the whole of Freud's teaching may be found in *The Marriage of Heaven and Hell.*[81] If that goes too far, the underlying point is well made. The more we learn, say, about the impact of Schopenhauer or Nietzsche on our century the more we find which we might otherwise have thought purely Freudian.[82] Freud's indebtedness to nineteenth-century German philosophy is only now becoming apparent.

For a related reason, the effort to plot the courses Freudianism has taken must also give due weight to the more general history of ideas. We have been taught by Philip Rieff to speak of 'the emergence of psychological man'. We have given him a name – and a set of attributes – but not a habitation. Naturally, a broad contrast can be drawn between psychological man and his communist counterpart – for whom, since Stalin and the Chinese Revolution, the prevailing psychiatry has normally been a punitive Pavlovianism. But the history of 'Freud's French Revolution' shows how much that simple contrast leaves unsaid about the specific conditions, intellectual and sociological, in which a genuine psychoanalytic culture arises.[83] The emergence of psychological man cannot be taken for granted.

Nor, of course, should his demise. From some perspectives psychoanalysis might seem to have withered in the face of the plentiful empirical and philosophical onslaughts that have been directed against it.[84] But the possible weakness of the discipline itself does not necessarily invalidate all examples of its heuristic application; these too demand appraisal. Like Marxism, psychoanalysis is a monument we cannot erase. To compare Freud with other significant psychologists of our age – Jung, Piaget, Pavlov, Skinner, Eysenck, the Gestalt school – is to be struck once again by how much

[81] 'Psychology and art today', *The English Auden*, ed. Edward Mendelson (London, 1977), p.339.

[82] See now Bryan Magee, *The Philosophy of Schopenhauer* (Oxford, 1983). Cf. Erich Heller, 'Observations about psychoanalysis and modern literature', *In the Age of Prose* (Cambridge, 1984).

[83] Cf. the works cited in notes 11 and 15 above; *Psychoanalysis, Creativity and Literature: An Anglo-French Enquiry*, ed. Alan Roland (New York, 1978); and Philip Rieff, *The Triumph of the Therapeutic* (New York, 1968).

[84] Cf. Stannard, and B.A. Farrell, *The Standing of Psychoanalysis* (Oxford, 1981). Sebastiano Timpanaro, *The Freudian Slip* (London, 1976), is the most convincing single-handed refutation of one particular aspect of Freudian theory. J.M. Masson, *Freud: The Assault on Truth, Freud's Suppression of the Seduction Theory* (London, 1984), is the latest *ad hominem* attack.

more Freud has had to offer. Throughout the English and German-speaking worlds the psychoanalysis of culture is, admittedly, unfashionable. Consciously or not, most accounts of human behaviour rehearse Durkheim's methodological postulate: 'every time a social phenomenon is directly explained by a psychological phenomenon, we may rest assured that the explanation is false.'[85] To use psychoanalysis under these circumstances is always to make a special case; and that remains true even if it is the general form rather than the specific content of Freud's ideas that is pressed into service.[86] Yet psychoanalysis is never beyond resuscitation, whether as a useful fiction, the greatest of modern myths, or as the queen of sciences. There may for all we know be further revolutions like that in France, and they may be founded on yet more surprising intellectual alliances.

At best, Freud's is 'perhaps the most important body of work committed to paper in the twentieth century', a worthy successor to Darwin's. At worst, extending a comparison drawn by a trenchant critic, it may be like Homer's stories of Olympus – masterly but unscientific.[87] To be compared to Homer even in failure is no bad thing.

[85] Emile Durkheim, *The Rules of Sociological Method*, ed. Steven Lukes (London, 1982), p.129.

[86] Cf. Meredith Anne Skura, *The Literary Use of the Psychoanalytic Process* (New Haven and London, 1981); Peter Gay, *Art and Act: On Causes in History – Manet, Gropius, Mondrian* (New York and London, 1976).

[87] Rieff, *Freud*, p.x; Karl R. Popper, *Realism and the Aim of Science* (London, 1983), p.172.

CHAPTER ONE

Symbolism, Imagination and Biological Destiny

Charles Rycroft

Some forty years ago I trained as a Freudian psychoanalyst. Since then I have been practising a form of therapy which other people, perhaps rightly, insist upon calling psychoanalysis, and I have from time to time written books and articles which can be construed as either contributions to or criticisms of psychoanalysis. The uncertainty, which exists as much in my mind as in anyone else's, arises from the fact that there is no such thing as psychoanalysis, in the sense of a clearly defined set of ideas and techniques which are universally agreed to constitute psychoanalysis, and which are held and practised by everyone who calls himself a psychoanalyst and by no one else.

If there were such a clearly-defined set of psychoanalytical ideas, it would be an easy matter to locate what influence psychoanalysis has had, and still is having, on the arts and humanities, and then, perhaps, to appraise whether that influence has been beneficial or baneful; but in fact, of course, things are not like that at all. Once upon a time it may have been possible to define as psychoanalytical any idea conceived, held and propagated by Freud and his immediate circle. But now, in the 1980s, seventy years after the quarrel between Freud and Jung, fifty years after the British Psychoanalytical Society began to be influenced by Melanie Klein, whom the Viennese analysts all regarded as a dangerous heretic, and over twenty years since existential analysis began to be imported into the English-speaking world by Laing,[1] Rollo May[2] and others, it has become difficult if not impossible to define precisely what this psychoanalysis is that has had an influence on the arts and humanities – and also, incidentally, on journalism and advertising.

When, fifteen years ago, I was rash enough to attempt a dictionary definition of psychoanalysis,[3] I followed usual Freudian practice in listing 'the unconscious', 'resistance', and 'transference' as its key defining concepts, but I felt it necessary to add that the general public insisted on using the word psychoanalysis to embrace all Freudian, Jungian and Adlerian ideas. Today, I would add that I think that the general public has been right to extend the meaning of the word psychoanalysis in this way, to ignore the differences between various schools and to be more impressed by their similarities. That much more goes on in our minds than most people are most of the time aware of, that we not uncommonly resist the emergence into consciousness of uncomfortable and disturbing thoughts, and that our present relationships are profoundly influenced by past ones – this set of ideas has, as W.H. Auden pointed out really before it happened,[4] become 'a whole climate of opinion', a way of looking at ourselves so pervasive that anyone not influenced by it is more likely to be resisting it than oblivious of it.

The ideas must, I think, be regarded as having had a beneficial effect on the arts and humanities, and indeed on our general experience of living, since they add enrichment, depth and resonance to our every perception of ourselves and others. But it must be remembered that the poem in which Auden asserted of Freud that 'to us he is no more a person/now but a whole climate of opinion' also contains the line, 'if often he was wrong and, at times, absurd'; and there are, I believe, still in circulation a number of specifically Freudian ideas which confuse rather than enlighten and which, when applied to the arts and humanities, have a diminishing, reductionist and disparaging effect. Historically speaking, these are ideas which Freud absorbed from the rationalist, medical world in

[1] R.D. Laing, *The Divided Self* (London, 1960); *The Self and Others* (London, 1961).

[2] *Psychology and the Human Dilemma* (Princeton, N.J., 1967).

[3] *A Critical Dictionary of Psychoanalysis* (London, 1968).

[4] 'In memory of Sigmund Freud', *Collected Poems*, ed. Edward Mendelson (London, 1976), p.217.

which he grew up and worked. I refer here specifically to two ideas that Freud held and built into his theories, though I doubt whether he can have consistently followed either of them in his practice. These are, first, that psychoanalysis is a natural science, no different in principle from say, physics and chemistry, and, secondly, that it is legitimate to use pathological phenomena as paradigms of normal experience.

The first led him to construct a model of the mind which was based on a mechanical, neuroanatomical metaphor, in which the actions, thoughts, feelings and aspirations of real, live people were conceptualized as though they were movements of energy within and between the various parts of what he called the psychic apparatus – these movements of energy being assumed to be as causally determined as are chemical reactions or the workings of a physical apparatus. It also led him to write *as though* he observed the workings of his patients' psychic apparatuses from an external, detached, objective and indeed superior position, when in fact he must have been conversing with them. I say 'as though' he was observing his patients' mental processes, since evidence derived from the memoirs of ex-patients and from his own asides shows that in fact he chatted with patients, addressed them by nicknames, sometimes complimented them on their insight, and made friends with several of them. However, the point I am trying to make here is that Freud, out of loyalty to the idea that psychoanalysis must be a natural science, constructed a language for talking about people which could not but dehumanize them – people after all are not apparatuses – and which not only omitted but even actively excluded any conception of an agent or self who creates or generates meaningful activity. This language, when applied to writers, artists and politicians, as it is in that curious genre of writing, 'pathobiography', turns out to have disastrous consequences: at the end of reading a pathobiography the reader is liable to have lost respect both for the author and for the subject. Having said this, it would be invidious for me to cite examples, but I cannot resist the temptation to mention that Freud has himself been the subject-victim of a pathobiography.[5]

While on the subject of psychoanalytical biographies it is perhaps worth mentioning that there is an essential difference between the

[5] Max Schur, *Freud: Living and Dying* (New York, 1972).

relationship of an analyst to his patient and that of a biographer to his subject. The patient is a voluntary participant in the therapeutic process and can reply to his analyst's interpretations, while the subject of a biography is a passive victim who cannot. An analyst and his patient may spend hundreds of hours closeted together; interaction and communication take place between them; and the analyst's ultimate criterion of the truth of his interpretations is that the patient finds them convincing – at any rate in the long run. But an entirely different state of affairs exists between the analytical biographer-critic and his subject-victim. Although the former may have unlimited access to his subject's paintings, writings, letters, and to the various memoirs, reminiscences and conventional biographies that may already have been written about him, he has no feedback from his subject himself. The interpretations the analyst-critic makes are in no sense the result of mutual endeavour, as are those that emerge at the end of a successful analysis. The analyst-critic is deprived of the critical monitoring that would have been forthcoming if his subject had really lain on his couch and been in a position to comment and answer – and answer back.

The second specifically Freudian idea which is still current, and which must be considered as having had a harmful effect, is that pathological phenomena can legitimately be regarded as paradigms of normal behaviour. This has led, and still leads, people to suppose, for instance, that since anxiety is often a neurotic symptom it always is, and that the perfect, healthy person would never on any occasion be anxious – not even when placed in totally unfamiliar surroundings or when confronting himself with some unusually testing task. It also, as Dr Storr shows, led Freud to believe – although he eventually abandoned the idea – that it should be possible to explain the creativeness of artists and writers by treating imaginative activity as though it were the same sort of thing as the neurotic, infantile, perverse fantasies that he was discovering in his patients. Instead of assuming, as most people educated in the arts and humanities do, that imagination is a basic human activity, faculty or function, which flowers more or less fruitfully in different people and different social and cultural settings, and that neurotic fantasies are perversions, distortions and restrictions of the imagination, Freud and the early analysts had the idea that they could explain imaginative activity by treating it as though it were the same thing as – as though it were nothing more than – neurotic fantasy. As a result, papers were written by Freud and others attempting to show that the artist, like the neurotic, is a day-dreamer; that the artist, like the neurotic, is reacting to infantile traumata; and, later, when many analysts became interested in depression, that the artist is making reparation for the destructive fantasies with which, as a depressive, he is burdened. And since day-dreaming, infantile traumata and destructive fantasies are ubiquitous, it was not difficult to find plausible examples appearing to confirm such explanations of the origin of creative, imaginative activity.

But, characteristically, such explanations confined themselves to establishing connections between the content of works of art and the artist's presumed infantile fantasies and traumata, and they failed to address themselves to the specifically aesthetic issues raised by imaginative activity: the nature and origin of the artist's and writer's ability to organize his imaginings into forms or patterns that feel 'right' to him and are satisfying to others; and to transmute personal experience and private imaginings into objects of public and universal appeal.

Psychoanalysts have, it seems to me, nothing to say about these two issues, the reason being, I suspect, that analogous issues do not in fact arise in the course of analytical practice. Analysts do not have to concern themselves with the presence or absence of formal patterns in the associations, fantasies and memories recounted to them by their patients, and they are employed by their patients to relieve disabilities and inhibitions, not to dissect the subtleties of creative functioning; it seems to be generally agreed that well-functioning capacities and 'sublimations' not only do not require analysis but are also unanalysable. Analysts therefore know more about why people have hang-ups and inhibitions than why they can be creative. And although analysts may spend a lot of time and energy helping their patients to find words to match their inchoate feelings, success in doing so falls far short of enabling them to universalize their personal experiences and imaginings.

It must have been considerations of this kind that led Freud to say in 1928 that 'before the problem of the creative artist analysis must, alas, lay down its arms'.[6] It is, however, perhaps worth considering

[6] 'Dostoevsky and parricide', *SE*, 21.177.

for a moment the implications of that 'alas, lay down its arms'. It betrays an imperialist streak in Freudian thinking, which assumes that Freud and the other Founding Fathers had discovered truths of such overwhelming and novel importance that they would be able to explain everything about human nature, and that psychoanalysis was going to have pervasive and revolutionary effects on all the arts and humanities – the possibility of a creative traffic in the opposite direction being scarcely envisaged. With the years this imperialist, expansionist tendency in the psychoanalytical movement seems to be diminishing. Professional biographers and historians have got to work on Freud and the early history of psychoanalysis and have shown that the early analysts were not quite as original as they seem to have thought they were; and it has become apparent that psychoanalysis is itself influenced by developments in other sciences and in the arts and humanities. But, none the less, I should still be somewhat surprised if a psychoanalytical college were to choose as its theme for a series of lectures the arts and the humanities and their influence on psychoanalysis. But, as we shall see, such an influence there has been.

There is an anecdote which illustrates some of the points I have been making. Some thirty years ago I was attending a conference of psychoanalysts at Geneva and sought relief from the profundities of the learned papers I was listening to in the daytime by reading a detective story in the evening. The one I chose was Wilkie Collins's *The Moonstone*. However, while, as I imagined, I was relaxing from the strenuous labours of the day, psychoanalytical thinking intruded itself on my reading and I became convinced that the Moonstone of the story was a Freudian symbol for the female genitals and that its theft, the crime of the story, symbolized loss of virginity. When the conference was over and I returned to London, I pursued my hunch and, not surprisingly, I discovered no evidence at all to suggest that Wilkie Collins had suffered any infantile trauma which might have left him unconsciously preoccupied with virginity; Collins was born in 1824 and such matters are in any case only rarely documented. But I also discovered extremely convincing evidence that as an adult he had, for a while at least, been consciously preoccupied with virginity and defloration. Sixteen years before writing *The Moonstone* he had written another novel, *Basil*, which has as its explicit theme the defloration of a virgin wife by someone who is not her husband.

Now it may be that when Collins wrote *The Moonstone* he was still preoccupied with virginity and that the theme re-emerged in symbolic form; but maybe, on the other hand, there is something adventitious and coincidental about the resemblance between the overt theme of one novel and the presumptive covert theme of the other – and in any case nineteenth-century men must in general have been more aware of virginity as a stealable property than we are nowadays. In some odd way, then, my psychoanalytical hunch or hypothesis had been simultaneously proved and disproved. And the aesthetics of the case was disconcerting too. *Basil*, the novel with the overt sexual theme, is dreadfully bad, while both T.S. Eliot and Dorothy Sayers regarded *The Moonstone* as the finest detective story in the English language.[7]

It will have become apparent that I think assessment of the influence of psychoanalysis on the arts and humanities to be complicated and confused by a contradiction within psychoanalysis itself. On the one hand it arose as a form of medical treatment which claimed to cure sick people of illnesses, and its findings were formulated in terms of a scientific model which assumed that the laws of causation applied to mental activity just as they do to physical phenomena. But, on the other hand, its data all derive from a personal relationship, albeit a very peculiar one, between two people – in which the therapist does not, indeed cannot, just observe mental processes going on in the patient's head and then assign causes to them, but has to use his imagination to empathize with his patient, and to discover the various additional concealed meanings contained in the overt text of what the patient says to him. As a result, there is a contradiction between a theory which categorizes mental events as 'phenomena' that can be observed and that have causes, and a practice which regards mental activity as the creation of an agent who generates meanings in everything he says and does – and who, characteristically, generates more meanings than he is, at the moment of generation, aware of.

Now this contradiction is widely, though not universally recognized by analysts themselves, though they speak more often of divorces, gaps and discrepancies between theory and practice than of

[7] See my 'The analysis of a detective story', in *Imagination and Reality* (London, 1968).

contradictions. However, André Green,[8] the French analyst, talks of 'confusions at the very heart of psychoanalysis', while Thomas Szasz, the American analyst, has declared mental illness to be a myth, and argues that psychoanalysis is a semantic theory and should be categorized as a moral not a natural science.[9] And Roy Schafer, another American analyst, is at present reformulating psychoanalytical theory in what he calls 'action language', based on the assumption that psychoanalysis is one of the humanities and that its central conception is *the person as agent* – an agent whose actions have meanings, who does things because he has reasons for doing them not because he is impelled to do them.[10] Leaning heavily on Oxford philosophers, notably Gilbert Ryle, Schafer argues that actions do not have causes, are not propelled by forces or impulses located in the id or the ego or anywhere else, for the simple reason that the forces and structures postulated by classical Freudian theory do not in fact exist. They are merely abstract nouns, and one is guilty of the logical fallacy of reification if one adduces them as causes. Nor is there really any place or structure called the mind or the psychic apparatus within which forces, drives, instincts, ids, egos, and super-egos can be located.

Now this 'action language' version of psychoanalysis certainly is an example of influence by the humanities, and it can indeed be taken as evidence that psychoanalysis is on its way to becoming one of them. However, if it does so, and if it is to avoid letting a number of babies out with the bath water, it will have to reformulate in humanistic terms several insights and concepts which to date have remained firmly embedded in classical Freudian language. It was to some of these that I was referring when I gave this lecture its portentous title, 'Symbolism, Imagination and Biological Destiny'.

According to classical Freudian theory there exists a class of symbols, most easily observed in dreams, which stand for bodily, mostly sexual, organs and processes; and repressed impulses achieve disguised, hallucinatory fulfilment by using these symbols to, as it were, fool the censorship imposed by the proprieties of consciousness. Furthermore, the theory holds that such Freudian symbols are

[8] Peter Fuller, 'A chat of analysts', *New Society*, 31 July 1975.
[9] *The Myth of Mental Illness* (London, 1962).
[10] *A New Language for Psychoanalysis* (New Haven and London, 1976).

constructed by movements of energy within the psychic apparatus, the two movements in question being displacement, by which energy moves from one mental image to another, and condensation, by which energy invested in several images is concentrated on one.

I doubt whether in a single paragraph I can give an account of the Freudian theory of symbolism that is either accurate or fair. But the point I wish to make here is that this theory contains insights of paramount importance to the arts and humanities, though this only becomes evident after one has translated the theory out of the language of natural science used by Freud into, I am tempted to say, ordinary English. One can then appreciate that Freud's statements about the movements of mental energy from one image to another are really statements about how we endow and attribute meanings to the objects we perceive and construct images of; and that what psychoanalysis has discovered is that human beings, presumably unlike other animals, think, imagine and dream in metaphor, seeing similarities between their own bodies and activities on the one hand and objects and processes perceived in the outside world on the other

As Marion Milner[11] in particular has pointed out, there seems to be a general, innate tendency to apprehend all objects that are not one's self by likening them to bodily organs and processes that are one's self, a tendency that enables us to assimilate the originally alien outside world into the inevitably and primordially familiar world of our own bodies and its sensations, and that provides us with a stock of images which we can liken to our own bodies and activities and to which our own bodies and activities can be likened. Imagery derived from our own body is thus available for making metaphorical, symbolic statements about the outside world – and about our own mental processes – and imagery derived from the outside world is available for making metaphorical, symbolic statements about ourselves, about our physical and mental states. In other words, there is a two-way imaginative traffic between our own body and its activities on the one hand and objects in the outside world on the other, so that each provides metaphors to describe the other.

I have spelled out in detail elsewhere[12] this idea that one of the,

[11] 'Aspects of symbolism in comprehension of the not-self', *International Journal of Psycho-Analysis*, 33 (1952).

[12] *The Innocence of Dreams* (London, 1979).

perhaps the, most important discovery of psychoanalysis is that man is a symbolizing animal who constructs on the foundation of his elemental bodily experiences a network of images which embraces and orders all his perceptions of the outside world. This network, or rather the construction of this network, is, I conceive, what we call imagination. It enables us to do not only what all other animals can do, that is react adaptively to the immediate present, but also to anticipate and rehearse the future, to re-live the past – as Bartlett pointed out years ago, remembering is an imaginative not a reproductive activity – to conceive how it would be to be someone else, to imagine how things could be other than they are, and to construct fictive alternative worlds. For the last two hundred and fifty years or so, this last use of the imagination has enjoyed a special status in our society, and there are indeed people who would restrict the word 'imagination' to mean solely the capacity to create original works of art.

Finally, I must turn to the last term in my title, biological destiny, and while doing so I shall draw attention to, and, I hope, dispel a popular misconception about psychoanalysis that has had a bad and misleading effect. This is the idea that, according to Freud, all symbols are sexual – hence, of course, the popular cant phrase, 'Freudian symbol'.

Now the statement that most symbols occurring in dreams are sexual can indeed be found in Freud's writing, but the passage in which it occurs turns out, on close inspection, to contain a category error, and once this error is eliminated Freud and psychoanalysis are revealed as saying something much more momentous than the popular idea that all dreams are sexual.

The crucial passage occurs in Freud's tenth *Introductory Lecture on Psycho-Analysis* of 1916[13] where he says: 'the range of things which are given symbolic representation in dreams is not wide: the human body as a whole, parents, children, brothers and sisters, birth, death, nakedness – and something else besides'. This 'something else besides' turns out to be the field of 'sexual life – the genitals, sexual processes, sexual intercourse. The very great majority of symbols in dreams are sexual symbols. And here a strange disproportion is revealed. The topics I have mentioned are few, but the symbols for

[13] *SE*, 15.153.

them are extremely numerous'. Freud then goes on to list over thirty symbols for the male genitals and over twenty for the female.

Now reading or hearing this quotation, and indeed the whole lecture from which it is taken, it is easy to conclude that Freud thought that in sleep at least we are all obsessed by sex, but once one has spotted that there is something very peculiar about his categories the picture changes significantly. In the first place Freud says that 'the range of things which are given symbolic representation in dreams is not wide', but then goes on to give a list of things – the body, parents, children, brothers and sisters, birth, death, nakedness, and that something else besides – which covers an extremely wide range of human experience, in fact almost everything apart from work, play and intellectual activity. And in the second place, by calling 'the field of sexual life' 'something else besides', he puts sex into a different category from the other items of his list, when in fact it has intimate connections with them all. Indeed so far from being 'something else besides' it is precisely what links together all the other things symbolized. After all, to go through Freud's list: we only have a body because our parents had sexual intercourse, at least once; we only have brothers and sisters because (or if) our parents had sexual intercourse more than once; birth and death are the first and last members of the series of birth, copulation and death; and nakedness has obvious connections with sex, birth and death.

So, if one refuses to follow Freud in his categorization of sex as something else besides, it becomes possible to reformulate his statements about symbolism in more general, inclusive terms, without in any way bowdlerizing them. It becomes possible to say that the range of things symbolized in dreams embraces all aspects of man's life-cycle, and that the psychoanalytical study of dreams reveals that human beings are more preoccupied than they mostly realize with their biological destiny – to use the widest term possible to encompass the whole life-cycle of birth, growth, love, reproduction, ageing and death. And this life-cycle has to be called destiny, however portentous the word sounds, because it is determined only marginally by conscious choices and decisions, but mainly by biological patterns that are inborn and ineluctable (e.g. innate vitality, temperament, aptitudes, age of onset of puberty and ageing), and by social factors over which we have had no choice. We did not choose our parents or select which genes they should pass on to us, nor the culture into which we were born, nor the impact upon us of the various social, economic and intellectual movements at work within that culture.

CHAPTER TWO

Psychoanalysis and Creativity

Anthony Storr

Although Freud's writings upon art and artists constitute a comparatively small fraction of his total output, the editors of the English *Standard Edition* list twenty-two references to writings 'dealing mainly or largely with Art, Literature or the theory of Aesthetics'.[1] Freud's papers on 'Leonardo da Vinci', on 'The Moses of Michelangelo' and on 'Dostoevsky and parricide' will be known to every student of his work.

There is no doubt that Freud had a deep appreciation, and love, of poetry and other forms of literature. His schooling had made him familiar with the Latin and Greek classics, and, throughout his life, he read widely, not only in German, but also in English, French, Italian and Spanish. After Freud had abandoned neuropathology for the study and treatment of neuroses, his writings contain far more references to novelists and playwrights, more especially to Shakespeare and to Goethe, than to the writings of other psychiatrists.

Freud's own talent as a writer was recognized early in his life. When he was only seventeen, he wrote to his friend Emil Fluss:

> At the same time my professor told me – and he is the first person who ventured to tell me this – that I had what Herder so neatly calls an 'idiotic' style, i.e. a style at once correct and characteristic. I was duly surprised at this amazing fact and hasten to spread the news of this happy event abroad as far and wide as possible – the first of its kind. To

[1] *SE*, 21.213-14.

you, for instance, who, I am sure, have until now not been aware that you are exchanging letters with a German stylist. So now I would counsel you, as a friend, not as one with a vested interest – preserve them – bind them together – guard them well – you never know.[2]

In 1930, Freud became the fourth recipient of the Goethe prize for Literature awarded by the City of Frankfurt. He could hardly have written so well himself if he had been unable to appreciate style in literature, but his aesthetic appreciation of the other arts was far more limited. Music, for example, was actually distasteful to him. When Freud was a boy, his sister Anna began to have music lessons. But the sound of her practising disturbed the studies of the *Wunderkind* and Freud's parents had the offending piano removed from the apartment. Freud's own children were not allowed to pursue music in the home, and his nephew Harry wrote of him: 'he despised music and considered it solely as an intrusion ... He never went to a concert and hardly to the theatre'.[3] Had Freud been musical, he would have been forced to pay more attention to aesthetic form, since the content of music cannot be verbally defined with any precision, whilst its effect, at any rate in classical music, is highly dependent upon the forms chosen by the composer. However, as Freud modestly acknowledged in his paper on 'The Moses of Michelangelo', aesthetic form remained a puzzle to him.

I may say at once that I am no connoisseur in art, but simply a layman. I have often observed that the subject-matter of works of art has a stronger attraction for me than their formal and technical qualities, though to the artist their value lies first and foremost in these latter. I am unable rightly to appreciate many of the methods used and the effects obtained in art. I state this so as to secure the reader's indulgence for the attempt I propose to make here.

Nevertheless, works of art do exercise a powerful effect on me, especially those of literature and sculpture, less often of painting. This has occasioned me, when I have been contemplating such things, to spend a long time before them trying to apprehend them in my own way, i.e. to explain to myself what their effect is due to. Wherever I

[2] Freud, 'Some early unpublished letters', *International Journal of Psycho-Analysis*, 50 (1969), p.425.

[3] Harry Freud, 'My Uncle Sigmund', in *Freud as We Knew Him*, ed. Hendrik M. Ruitenbeek (Detroit, 1973), p.313.

> cannot do this, as for instance with music, I am almost incapable of obtaining any pleasure. Some rationalistic, or perhaps analytic, turn of mind in me rebels against being moved by a thing without knowing why I am thus affected and what it is that affects me.
>
> This has brought me to recognize the apparently paradoxical fact that precisely some of the grandest and most overwhelming creations of art are still unresolved riddles to our understanding. We admire them, we feel overawed by them, but we are unable to say what they represent to us. I am not sufficiently well-informed to know whether this fact has already been remarked upon; possibly, indeed, some writer on aesthetics has discovered that this state of intellectual bewilderment is a necessary condition when a work of art is to achieve its greatest effects. It would only be with the greatest reluctance that I could bring myself to believe in any such necessity.[4]

Freud's disclaimer was not false modesty. His lack of aesthetic appreciation of the visual arts is attested from another source. Freud was a passionate collector of antiquities, especially of Roman, Etruscan, Assyrian and Egyptian statuettes. In May 1938, a few days before Freud's journey to England from Nazi-occupied Vienna on June 4th, the photographer Edmund Engelman recorded for posterity the appearance of that famous apartment at Berggasse 19.[5] Freud's consulting room and study are overflowing with an unbelievable number of antique statuettes, crowded together so closely that the outline of any individual piece is hardly discernible. These are not the rooms of an aesthete, but those of a compulsive collector. Freud once told Jung that, were he to suffer from a neurosis, it would be of obsessional type. His accumulation of objects and the manner in which he arranged them bears this out.

Freud's principal interest, therefore, was in the subject-matter of works of art, not in the skill, style, or manner in which they were presented. In *An Autobiographical Study*, Freud wrote that analysis 'can do nothing toward elucidating the nature of the artistic gift, nor can it explain the means by which the artist works – artistic technique'.[6] And in his paper on Dostoevsky, as Dr Rycroft reminds us, he wrote: 'before the problem of the creative artist analysis must, alas, lay down its arms'.[7]

[4] *SE*, 13.211-12.
[5] Edmund Engelman, *Berggasse 19* (New York, 1976).
[6] *SE*, 20.65.
[7] *SE*, 21.177.

Since content, rather than style, was the problem to which Freud addressed himself, it was reasonable that he should apply the same method of interpretation to works of art as he did to dreams, fantasies and neurotic symptoms. The subjects which an artist selects, and the ways in which he chooses to present those subjects are, of course, partly dictated by the conventions of his time. But his choices are also determined partly by his personality and by his personal history, even though, in some instances, he may himself be unconscious of the connection.

As an example of Freud's procedure, one cannot do better than turn to his essay on Leonardo. In recent years, this monograph of 1910 has been somewhat discredited, since Freud's interpretation of a fantasy memory of Leonardo's, in which a bird is supposed to have struck his lips with its tail, has been shown to be based upon a mistranslation. The bird was a kite and not a vulture; and whereas vultures can be shown to have mythological connections with the mother, kites cannot. However, this error of Freud's does not invalidate the other interpretations which he advances.

Freud is careful to point out that he does not regard Leonardo as a neurotic, although he suggests that he may have had some obsessional traits of character. On the basis of slender information, Freud nevertheless builds up a convincing explanation of Leonardo's homosexual orientation. Leonardo was an illegitimate child, and for his first few years lived only with his mother. Freud supposes, with reason, that the absence of a father combined with the excessive caresses of a lonely mother might well have made heterosexuality difficult of achievement. When Freud comes to discuss Leonardo's paintings, what interests him is the presumed relation of their content to the circumstances of Leonardo's childhood. The famous, ambiguous smile which appears on the faces of some of Leonardo's subjects is traced back to a presumedly similar smile on the face of the artist's mother; and the androgynous appearance of some of his portraits is attributed to Leonardo's homosexuality. Freud comments at some length upon the picture of the Virgin and Child with St Anne.[8] As many critics have observed, St Anne seems hardly older than her daughter, the Virgin Mary. Freud first notes that the subject of mother, grandmother and child may have suggested itself to Leonardo because, once he had been removed from the sole care

[8] *SE*, 11.59-137.

of his mother, he was brought up in a household which included his paternal grandmother as well as his stepmother. Freud goes on to suggest that the similarity in age between the Virgin and St Anne may be a reflection of the fact that Leonardo did, in effect, have two mothers; his real mother and then his stepmother, who was also supposed to have been devoted to him. As it appears that this subject is one rarely chosen by artists, Freud's interpretations carry conviction. However, this method of interpretation can only be applied to representational art. What, one wonders, would Freud have said if he had been confronted by a canvas of Mark Rothko's? It can also be said, with justice, that Freudian interpretation always leads back to the artist's personality: that is, it may reveal something about the artist, but does not tell us much about the work of art itself.

It has sometimes been alleged that, because Freud used the same methods of interpretation for works of art as he did for neurotic symptoms, he did not distinguish between the two. But it must be remembered, as Richard Wollheim has pointed out in a lecture on 'Freud and the interpretation of art', that Freud was aiming at a general theory of how the mind works, and that his interpretation of art appears, at any rate at first sight, to be consistent with such a theory. We all express, in our speech and in our actions, desires and wishes of which we are only partially conscious, to which psychoanalytic interpretation can be applied. There is no reason to exclude works of art from this kind of scrutiny. In the Freudian scheme, works of art are regarded as being largely the result of sublimation; that is, of a mechanism by which instinctual impulses are diverted from direct expression and transformed into something more acceptable to society. Although sublimation is technically classified as a mechanism of defence, it is described by Anna Freud as pertaining 'more to the study of the normal than to that of neurosis'.[9] However, although sublimation is a mechanism of defence employed by normal people, Freud was evidently of the opinion that artists needed to, or were driven to, employ sublimation more than most of us, and were therefore closer to neurosis than the average. As late as 1917, in the twenty-third *Introductory Lecture on Psycho-Analysis*, Freud wrote:

[9] Anna Freud, *The Ego and the Mechanisms of Defence* (London, 1968), p.44.

An artist is once more in rudiments an introvert, not far removed from neurosis. He is oppressed by excessively powerful instinctual needs. He desires to win honour, power, wealth, fame and the love of women; but he lacks the means for achieving these satisfactions. Consequently, like any other unsatisfied man, he turns away from reality and transfers all his interest, and his libido too, to the wishful constructions of his life of phantasy, whence the path might lead to neurosis.[10]

Freud considered that fantasy was derived from play, and regarded both activities in a negative light since they were, in his view, a denial of, or turning away from, reality:

The growing child, when he stops playing, gives up nothing but the link with real objects; instead of *playing*, he now *phantasies*. He builds castles in the air and creates what are called *day-dreams*.[11]

The creative writer does the same as the child at play. He creates a world of phantasy which he takes very seriously – that is which he invests with large amounts of emotion – while separating it sharply from reality.[12]

Freud proceeds to consider the nature of fantasy.

We may lay it down that a happy person never phantasies, only an unsatisfied one. The motive forces of phantasies are unsatisfied wishes, and every single phantasy is the fulfilment of a wish, a correction of an unsatisfying reality.[13]

Although not every one who engages in fantasy becomes neurotic, and, as we shall see, creative people are a special case, because their creative abilities make it possible for them to link their fantasies with reality, fantasy is a dangerous activity. For 'neurotics turn away from reality because they find it unbearable – either the whole or parts of it.'[14]

Freud conceived that, at the beginning of life, the infant was

[10] *SE*, 16.376.
[11] *SE*, 9.145.
[12] *SE*, 9.144.
[13] *SE*, 9.146.
[14] *SE*, 12.218.

dominated by the pleasure principle and that the pleasures sought were entirely sensual in nature. From time to time, the Nirvana-like bliss of the satisfied infant would be disturbed by 'the peremptory demands of internal needs';[15] for food, for warmth and so on. Freud goes on:

> When this happened, whatever was thought of (wished for) was simply presented in a hallucinatory manner, just as still happens today with our dream-thoughts every night. It was only the non-occurrence of the expected satisfaction, the disappointment experienced, that led to the abandonment of this attempt at satisfaction by means of hallucination. Instead of it, the psychical apparatus had to decide to form a conception of the real circumstances in the external world and to endeavour to make a real alteration in them. A new principle of mental functioning was introduced; what was presented to the mind was no longer what was agreeable but what was real, even if it happened to be disagreeable. This setting-up of the *reality principle* proved to be a momentous step.[16]

So, fantasy is equated with hallucination, with dreaming, with turning away from reality, with the persistence of an infantile mode of mental functioning which Freud called 'primary process'. Proper adaptation to the external world is by means of deliberate thought and planning; by postponement of immediate satisfaction; by the abandonment of wish-fulfilling fantasy. Freud wrote:

> Art brings about a reconciliation between the two principles in a peculiar way. An artist is originally a man who turns away from reality because he cannot come to terms with the renunciation of instinctual satisfaction which it at first demands, and who allows his erotic and ambitious wishes full play in the life of phantasy. He finds a way back to reality, however, from this world of phantasy by making use of special gifts to mould his phantasies into truths of a new kind, which are valued by men as precious reflections of reality. Thus in a certain fashion, he actually becomes the hero, the king, the creator, or the favourite he desired to be, without following the long roundabout path of making alterations in the external world. But he can only achieve this because other men feel the same dissatisfaction as he does

[15] *SE*, 12.219.
[16] *SE*, 12.219.

with the renunciation demanded by reality, and because that dissatisfaction, which results from the replacement of the pleasure principle by the reality principle, is itself a part of reality.[17]

This is surely a strange conception of both art and artist. It implies that, though the artist wins out in the end, and may even escape neurosis, his art is still an indirect way of obtaining satisfactions which, if he was fully adapted to reality, would be unnecessary. Even those who admire and enjoy what the artist has produced are still turning away from reality in the direction of fantasy. The implication must be that art is primarily escapist and that, in an ideal world in which everyone had matured sufficiently to replace the pleasure principle by the reality principle, there would be no place for art.

Yet, in an earlier paper Freud had written:

> But creative writers are valuable allies and their evidence is to be prized highly, for they are apt to know a whole host of things between heaven and earth of which our philosophy has not yet let us dream. In their knowledge of the mind they are far in advance of us everyday people, for they draw upon sources which we have not yet opened up for science.[18]

This is, perhaps, not quite such a positive view of the artist as it appears, since Freud is hinting that, once the sources upon which the artist draws have been opened up by science, so much will be known about the mind that the creative writer's art will not be needed. This is borne out by what Freud says about science in that same paper on the two principles of mental functioning from which I have already quoted. After noting that religions, also, advocate the postponement of immediate satisfaction, Freud writes:

> *Religions* have been able to effect absolute renunciation of pleasures in this life by means of the promise of compensation in a future existence; but they have not by this means achieved a conquest of the pleasure principle. It is *science* which comes nearest to succeeding in that conquest; science too, however, offers intellectual pleasures during its work and promises practical gain in the end.[19]

[17] *SE*, 12.224.
[18] *SE*, 9.8.
[19] *SE*, 12.223-4.

So science is to be equated with the abandonment of fantasy; with postponement of immediate satisfaction; with 'secondary process' mental functioning; with thinking that is adapted to reality. Freud states that thinking acts as a restraint upon discharge.

> Thinking was endowed with characteristics which made it possible for the mental apparatus to tolerate an increased tension of stimulus whilst the process of discharge was postponed. It is essentially an experimental kind of acting, accompanied by displacement of relatively small quantities of cathexis together with less expenditure (discharge) of them.[20]

Freud also wrote: 'it is one of the principal functions of our thinking to master the material of the external world psychically'.[21]

Freud was certainly right in assuming that intellectual functioning is related to the ability to postpone responses to immediate stimuli. David Stenhouse, in his book on *The Evolution of Intelligence*, defines intelligent behaviour as 'behaviour that is adaptively variable within the lifetime of the individual'.[22] The lower we descend down the evolutionary scale, the more likely we are to find that behaviour is not variable, but rather consists of preprogrammed, rigid, invariable responses to incoming stimuli. Stenhouse suggests that, if the evolution of intelligent behaviour is to occur,

> the most important factor is that which gives the individual animal the power not to respond in the usual way to the stimulus-situation which previously initiated an instinctive sequence culminating in a consummatory act. This power not to respond may be absolute, or may be merely the ability to delay the response – withhold it provisionally as it were – but its absence would negate the very possibility of adaptive variability in behaviour.[23]

But is scientific thinking really so removed from the sphere of fantasy as Freud assumes? It is clear that, if scientific hypotheses are to gain acceptance, they must be related to the real world, and be

[20] *SE*, 12.221.
[21] *SE*, 21.212.
[22] London, 1974, p.31.
[23] Stenhouse, p.67.

proven to increase our understanding of how the real world functions. Although science progresses by the refutation of hypotheses, and each scientific theory is ultimately supplanted by another which includes still more phenomena within its grasp, yet each theory has to be proven by experiment and shown to correspond with external reality. But proving a scientific hypothesis is secondary. Scientific thinking takes its origin from fantasy in exactly the same way as telling stories or any other creative activity. Einstein attributed his creative success not to his abilities as a mathematician and physicist, but to his imagination. Einstein's own attempt to define 'thinking' is worth quoting.

> What, precisely, is thinking? When at the reception of sense-impressions, memory pictures emerge, this is not yet 'thinking'. When, however, a certain picture turns up in many such series, then – precisely through such return – it becomes an ordering element for such series in that it connects series which in themselves are unconnected. Such an element becomes an instrument, a concept. I think that the transition from free association or 'dreaming' to thinking is characterized by the more or less dominating role which the 'concept' plays in it. It is by no means necessary that a concept must be connected with a sensorily cognizable and reproducible sign (word); but when this is the case thinking becomes by means of that fact communicable.[24]

Einstein goes on to say that thinking is 'a free play with concepts', and that the justification for this kind of thinking, far removed as it may still be from any consensus of what constitutes 'truth', is that in this way the thinker can emancipate himself from the experience of the senses. In his *Notes for an Obituary*, Einstein wrote: 'perception of this world by thought, leaving out everything subjective, became, partly consciously, partly unconsciously, my supreme aim'.[25] Einstein was sure that most thinking went on without the use of words and that it was, to a considerable degree, unconscious. Freud would have agreed with this part of Einstein's statement. Indeed, he wrote: 'it is probable that thinking was originally unconscious, in so far as it went beyond mere ideational presentations and was directed

[24] Jeremy Bernstein, *Einstein* (London, 1973), pp.39-40.
[25] Antonina Vallentin, *Einstein* (London, 1954), p.9.

to the relations between impressions of objects, and that it did not acquire further qualities, perceptible to consciousness, until it became connected with verbal residues'.[26] But Freud goes on to say:

> With the introduction of the reality principle one species of thought-activity was split off; it was kept free from reality-testing and remained subordinated to the pleasure-principle alone. This activity is *phantasying*, which begins already in children's play, and later, continued as *day-dreaming*, abandons dependence on real objects.[27]

But are not the greatest achievements of the human mind only possible because human beings are capable of abandoning dependence on real objects, in other words, capable of fantasy? Is not Einstein's definition of thinking as 'a free play with concepts' a form of what Freud pejoratively dismissed as fantasy? Freud treated fantasy as though it was always escapist, but this is not necessarily the case: nor is it true of dreams.

Freud, I believe, was never at ease when thinking strayed too far from the body and physical sensation, which seemed to him to constitute reality. Freudian interpretation always strives to reduce abstractions, such as the notion of beauty, to something physical. For example, Freud writes: 'there is to my mind no doubt that the concept of "beautiful" had its roots in sexual excitation and that its original meaning was "sexually stimulating" '.[28]

For Einstein, creative thinking had to be as far removed from sense impressions as possible, since he regarded the latter as unreliable. Einstein wrote: 'I believe that the first step in the setting up of a "real external world" is the formation of the concept of bodily objects of various kinds'. So far, Freud would have agreed with him. But Einstein goes on:

> The second step is to be found in the fact that, in our thinking (which determines our expectation), we attribute to this concept of the bodily object a significance, which is to a high degree independent of the sense impression which originally gives rise to it. This is what we mean when we attribute to the bodily object 'a real existence'. The

[26] *SE*, 12.221.
[27] *SE*, 12.222.
[28] *SE*, 7.156.

> justification of such a setting rests exclusively on the fact that, by means of such concepts and mental relations between them, we are able to orient ourselves in the labyrinth of sense impressions. These notions and relations, although free statements of our thoughts, appear to us as stronger and more alterable than the individual sense experience itself, the character of which as anything other than the result of an illusion or hallucination is never completely guaranteed.[29]

Einstein's new model of the universe depended upon his being able to emancipate himself from 'real objects'. Indeed, in order to conceive the special theory of relativity, he had to free himself from the subjective prejudice implicit in being a dweller upon earth, and imagine how the universe would appear to an observer travelling at near the speed of light. Is not this fantasy, albeit fantasy which was later shown by experiment to explain phenomena which did not fit in with Newton's model?

It might be affirmed that my disagreement with Freud is no more than a semantic issue. Perhaps he is using the word fantasy in one sense, whilst I am using it in another. It is certainly true that there are such things as escapist fantasies and idle day-dreams. These play their part in rather lowly forms of creative activity like 'romantic' fiction, or the James Bond novels of Ian Fleming. But not all fantasies are of this kind. Freud was convinced that all mental activity which was not dependent on 'real objects' was mere wish-fulfilment. Yet, just as play can be preparatory for, and hence directed toward, adult activities like fighting, hunting and sexual intercourse, so day-dreaming can also be a form of anticipatory practice. I have often day-dreamed about the formidable task of participating in this series of lectures, and my fantasies about your shafts of criticism and your expert scrutiny have made me more scrupulous in my presentation than I might otherwise have been.

Freud's theory of dreams is equally open to question. Freud was particularly enthusiastic about his dream theory. In his Preface to the third English edition of *The Interpretation of Dreams*, he wrote: 'insight such as this falls to one's lot but once in a lifetime'.[30] He even allowed himself the fantasy that, one day, a marble tablet would be placed on the house in which he first studied dreams

[29] *Out of My Later Years* (London, 1956), pp.60-1.
[30] *SE*, 4.xxxii.

seriously. This would read: 'Here the secret of dreams was revealed to Dr. Sigm. Freud on July 24, 1895'.[31] It is ironic that the discovery of which Freud was proudest does not withstand critical scrutiny. Freud's mature theory of dreams claims that every dream, even a nightmare or an anxiety dream, is an attempt to fulfil a wish; and that every dream represents a wish-fulfilment dating from early childhood as well as a wish-fulfilment from current mental life. Because these wishes were for the most part unacceptable, they appeared in dreams in disguised form. Hence, what the dreamer actually recalled was only the 'manifest content' of the dream. The true meaning of the dream, its so-called 'latent content', could only be revealed when the dreamer's associations to the images in the dream had been subjected to psychoanalytical scrutiny and interpretation.

The function of the dream, Freud believed, was to preserve sleep by giving disguised expression to wishes of an aggressive or sexual kind which, if they had been allowed to occur to the dreamer in undisguised form, would have been likely to have wakened him.

Although dreams are not couched in the language of everyday speech, there is really no evidence that all dreams are concealing something unacceptable. Nor is there sufficient reason to believe that all dreams represent unfulfilled wishes, although this is certainly true of some. Freud himself recognized that an exception had to be made when considering the dreams of people who have been subjected to some 'traumatic' incident, like an accident or an explosion. Such people often have dreams in which the incident itself recurs in undisguised form. Freud guessed that, in such cases, the dream might be an attempt at coming to terms with, or mastering, a disturbing stimulus; a way of looking at dreams which is actually more fruitful than Freud's original theory.

Jung, who co-operated with Freud for some years in the early 1900s, but who then parted company with him to found his own school, took a very different view of dreams. He did not consider that dreams were concealments, but rather that they were expressed in a symbolic language, which though it might be difficult to understand, was, in essence, a natural form of human expression. Poetry is another kind of human utterance in which symbol and metaphor

[31] Ernest Jones, *Sigmund Freud: Life and Work* (London, 1953-7), 1.388.

play a predominant role, but we do not think of most poetry as wilfully obscure on this account.

Dreams seem frequently to be concerned with unsolved problems. A man I knew once dreamed that he was looking into the window of a shop. Inside was a statuette of a beautiful woman standing upon a square base. Since both the statuette and its base were made of some translucent material, the dreamer could see that there were letters carved upon the underside of the base. He knew that what was written there was 'The Secret of Life'. But, because from his viewpoint, the letters were both upside down and the wrong way round, he could not read them. A dream with an extraordinarily similar theme is reported by Dr Rycroft in his book *The Innocence of Dreams.*[32] A man dreamed that he noticed in the window of an antique shop an old book which he knew contained 'The Truth'. On inquiring inside, he was told that the book was the only copy of an otherwise unknown work of Immanuel Kant. But it was written in a language which no one could understand.

These dreams do not provide solutions to the problems which they raise. Although most creative inspiration comes to people when they are in a state of reverie rather than actually asleep, there are a number of authentic instances of problem-solving during sleep, or of new ideas coming out of a dream. In one experiment, students were presented with a variety of difficult problems which they were required to study for fifteen minutes before going to sleep. Many had dreams related to the problems, and a few reported finding solutions. People have reported dreams in which a game of chess was played, an algebraic problem solved and a book-keeping error detected. Robert Louis Stevenson said that the plot of Dr Jekyll and Mr Hyde came to him in a dream; and the composer Tartini named a composition 'The Devil's Trill Sonata' because he had a dream in which the Devil took up a violin and played it to him.

Stanley Palombo, in his book *Dreaming and Memory,*[33] suggests that dreaming is a way of processing information. During the day, every one of us is exposed to a vast number of incoming stimuli and presented with a mass of 'information'. Only a small proportion of this information will be remembered, even for a short time, and still

[32] London, 1979, p.124.
[33] New York, 1978.

less will be transferred from the short-term memory system to the long-term memory store. However, our adaptation to the environment is largely dependent upon our being able to compare our current experience with our past experience, which is stored in the memory. It is the unfamiliar which engages our attention, whilst we take the familiar for granted; but we only recognize the unfamiliar as being so because we have a memory of what has gone before. Palombo thinks that dreams are one way in which the experience of the day is matched with the residues of previous experience before being assigned to the long-term memory.

This theory of dreams goes some way to explaining why it is that dreams so often seem to be such a curious mixture of events of the previous day with memories from the remote past. There is a kind of scanning process going on, perhaps selecting things which go together because they share a similar emotional tone rather than because they happened together in time.

If we try to put together these varying notions of dreams – that they are concerned with mastering disturbing experiences; that they are sometimes attempts at solving problems; and that they may be a way of processing information – we might hazard the proposition that dreams are in some way an attempt of the mind to order its own experience. This is borne out by the fact that so many dreams are cast in the form of a story which links together the various episodes of the dream, however absurd or incongruous these separate episodes may appear.

Many forms of play are also concerned with order. In his book *Homo Ludens*, Johan Huizinga, the Dutch historian, convincingly supposes that play is the primeval soil in which all cultural manifestations are rooted. Without play, we should have neither craft nor art, neither poetry nor music. Huizinga points out that

> in some languages the manipulation of musical instruments is called 'playing', to wit, in the Arabic language on the one hand and the Germanic and Slavonic on the other. Since this semantic understanding between East and West can hardly be ascribed to borrowing or coincidence, we have to assume some deep-rooted psychological reason for so remarkable a symbol of the affinity between music and play.[34]

[34] London, 1970, p.182.

Games, also, are a way of ordering experience. Games allow for the controlled expression and mastery of competitive and aggressive impulses within a structure of rules and defined area or framework like a playing-field.

So it appears that the three activities, play, fantasy and dreaming, which Freud linked together as escapist or hallucinatory, can equally well be regarded as adaptive; as attempts to come to terms with reality, rather than to escape from it; as ways of selecting from, and making new combinations out of, our experience of both the external world and the inner world of the psyche. None of these activities is as far removed from 'thinking' as they appeared to him; and, as we have seen, Freud considered that a principal function of thinking was to master the material of the external world psychically.

If Freud had been able to accept that play, fantasy and dreaming were attempts to come to terms with, and master, reality rather than to escape from it, he would not have had to lay down his arms before the problem of the creative artist nor have felt that the grandest creations of art were unsolved riddles to his understanding. Art and science, though very different activities, have certain aims in common. Both are concerned with seeking order in complexity, and unity in diversity. As the Gestalt psychologists were the first to affirm, the human tendency toward pattern-making is inborn and inescapable. We cannot see three dots but that we make them into a triangle. Human beings have to order their experience, both spatially and temporally, as part of their biological adaptation to reality, and the forces which impel them to do so are just as 'instinctive' as sex. Although Freud did not call it that, I am sure that he appreciated the aesthetic aspect of scientific discovery; the intense satisfaction which accompanies solving a problem, or inventing a new explanatory principle. The 'eureka' experience is a pleasure closely allied to aesthetic appreciation; for part of what we admire about a painting or a piece of music is the order which the artist has imposed upon what would otherwise have appeared disconnected or chaotic. The nearest Freud comes to acknowledging this kind of pleasure is in his book on jokes. Having recognized that all jokes are tendentious, that is, ways of expressing sexual or aggressive feelings, he reluctantly admits that the techniques of jokes are themselves sources of pleasure. When things which appear incongruous are linked together, Freud supposes that we are economizing our expenditure of psychic energy. This brings pleasure, but of a rather minor variety. Freud calls it a 'fore-pleasure'; that is, a slight pleasure which leads on to and makes possible a much greater pleasure. Freud supposes that the form in which writers dress up their fantasies is a kind of fore-pleasure or 'incentive bonus' designed to bribe the reader into enjoying something much deeper; the work's imaginative content, which the writer had to clothe in enticing form in order to make it acceptable.

Because Freud thought of the id as a chaotic cauldron of seething instincts entirely governed by the pleasure principle, in which form was notably lacking, he regarded the need to select, to order, and to impose form upon experience as predominantly a conscious, rational phenomenon. Modern psychoanalysts, particularly Marion Milner and Anton Ehrenzweig, have realized that the drive toward order arises unconsciously. Indeed, Ehrenzweig called his last, posthumously published book *The Hidden Order of Art.*[35]

Sir Ernst Gombrich, in his book *The Sense of Order*,[36] links man's need for pattern-making with his exploratory tendencies. In discovering more about our environment we create internal patterns or schemata. By doing so, we reduce the need to pay equal attention to every impinging stimulus, and only need to take notice of those stimuli which are novel; that is, those which do not fit in with our preformed schemata. A simple instance of this is descending a straight staircase. We only need to pay detailed attention to where it begins and ends, because we assume that each stair will be the same height and width as its fellows. Information theory, originally derived from practical work with telephone cables and other carriers of information, has thrown light on how we economize our intake by taking parts for wholes, and only pay attention to the unexpected. If we had no prior conception of regularity, we could not begin to make corrections to it; and if there were no regularities at all, our environment would be entirely unpredictable; a nightmare, as Gombrich calls it. One modern theory of schizophrenia suggests that sufferers lack some aspect of selective discrimination. Overwhelmed by stimuli which they can neither order nor disregard, they are compelled to withdraw as far as possible from the impact of the world.

[35] London, 1967.
[36] Oxford, 1979.

As we have seen, Freud's idea was that the motivation of the artist and the motivation of the scientist could be sharply distinguished. The driving force behind the artist's need to create was unsatisfied instinct, expressing itself originally in escapist fantasy. The driving force behind the scientist's activity (about which Freud says little) is to master the material of the external world psychically. I hope I have convinced you that these two creative activities have more in common than Freud supposed. Both artists and scientists are concerned with creating order, a basic drive or need which, because we share it, makes us able to appreciate, and perhaps envy, what the great creators achieve.

This way of looking at creative endeavour raises an obvious problem. If scientific and artistic creativity have so much in common, in what ways are they different? It is clear that a scientific hypothesis is not a work of art, nor is a work of art a scientific hypothesis.

Leonard Meyer, discussing this question in his paper 'Concerning the sciences, the arts, – AND the humanities,'[37] points out that scientists are discovering something which is already there, like the double helix, whereas artists create something which has never previously existed, like the C sharp minor quartet of Beethoven. We assume, with good reason, that the structure of the DNA molecule was, and always has been, the same. Watson and Crick did not create its structure, but discovered it. But nothing like the C sharp minor quartet existed before Beethoven composed it. He did not discover it; he created it.

Meyer goes on to point out that there is a temporal progress in science which makes even the greatest generalizations, like Newton's Law of Universal Gravitation, out of date. It follows that scientists have no need to study in detail the original papers of Newton or any other innovator, since their discoveries will have become part of the general scientific edifice.

The same is not true of works of art. Although styles change in the course of time, Beethoven is not an advance on Mozart, nor Picasso on Cézanne: they are simply different. Students of music and painting need to study all four. Meyer discusses a number of other differences which I need not pursue. What I am concerned with here is the similarity between the actual process of creative discovery as it

[37] *Critical Inquiry*, 1 (September 1974).

takes place in the mind of an artist and that in the mind of a scientist. A new scientific hypothesis and a new work of art have in common that both are the product of mental activity in which abstraction, fantasy and playing with various combinations of concepts all take part. Often, both are concerned with combining and transcending opposites. In another paper[38] I have taken as a scientific example Newton's synthesis between the discoveries of Kepler and those of Galileo which resulted in a theory which transcended both: the Law of Universal Gravitation. This is a classic example of how two sets of laws which were previously thought to be entirely separate could be both reconciled and superseded by a new hypothesis.

My example from the arts was Beethoven's 'Grosse Fuge', the movement originally designed as the final movement of the quartet in B flat, opus 130. Martin Cooper wrote of this:

> What grips the listener is the dramatic experience of forcing – for there is frequently a sense of violence in this mastery – two themes which have, by nature, nothing in common, to breed and produce a race of giants, episodes or variations that have no parallel in musical history.[39]

Newton's synthesis is concerned with the facts of the external world; Beethoven's with what he found in his internal world. It seems to me probable that the mental processes employed by each man of genius in seeking his solution were not dissimilar.

Whereas the scientist is pointed toward discovering order in the external world, the artist is directed toward creating order within: toward making sense out of his subjective experience. What points the scientist in one direction, the artist in the other, is still obscure – although Liam Hudson has thrown some light upon the subject in his studies of the temperamental differences between young people who choose the arts and those who choose the sciences as subjects of study. Both types of creativity are, I believe, motivated by a 'divine discontent' which is part of man's biological endowment. Mystery and disorder spur man to discovery, to the creation of new hypotheses which bring order and pattern to the maze of phenomena. But mystery and disorder pertain to our own natures as well as to the

[38] 'Individuation and the creative process', *Journal of Analytical Psychology*, 28 (1983).
[39] *Beethoven: The Last Decade* (Oxford, 1970), pp.388-9.

external world. I venture to suggest that, just as it is inconceivable that all the laws of Nature will ever be discovered, so it is equally impossible to believe that the complexities of human nature can ever be grasped in their entirety.

> Ah, but a man's reach should exceed his grasp,
> Or what's a heaven for?[40]

[40] Robert Browning, *Andrea del Sarto*, lines 97-8.

CHAPTER THREE

Freud and Literary Biography

Richard Ellmann

Although four lecturers in this series find fault with Freud, the series could hardly have come into being if the horse we were to flog was already quite dead. I should maintain that we are all still under Freud's long shadow. Last autumn in the United States I read in the press of a dreadful crime: a young man, egged on by his mother, murdered his father. The newspapers helpfully explained that the young man had a very prominent Oedipus complex. If we dismiss this as just a journalistic excess, and an American one to boot, we would do well to remember how hard it is to open our own mouths without registering the effect of Freud upon the language. We converse casually about the sexual proclivities of infants, about sibling rivalries, about dependency upon the mother, about sadomasochistic impulses. When we forget things we suspect ourselves of having wanted to forget them. We may shun the technical vocabulary of Freud, words such as ego, super-ego, id, the anal, oral, and genital stages, the pleasure principle and the reality principle, yet we are hardly likely to do without such words as aggression, anxiety, complex, compulsion, the unconscious, defence mechanism, narcissism, death wish, erogenous zones, fixation, guilt feeling, sublimation, wish-fulfilment. Freud may not have invented most of these words, yet he connected them together and he gave them a special colour and shape. And quite apart from terminology, Freud has given us the conviction that a secret life is going on within us which is only partly under our control.

Perhaps no part of society has been more disrupted by the coming of Freud than has the community of letters. During the nineteenth century, literature grew more and more in the habit of claiming autonomy as a privileged and separate subject. Words such as art and artistic took on an extraordinary dignity. Psychoanalysis has disrupted these pretensions in several distinct ways. First, it has argued that we are all, artists and non-artists, involved in the chronic production of symbolic fantasies, in dreams or day-dreams, in more or less directed oneirism. This being so, artists are not an élite, they are much like other people, at most Rembrandts when the rest of us are only Grandma Moseses. Second, psychoanalysis, an infant discipline, takes over from age-old literature terms such as Oedipus and Narcissus, and to some extent preempts them, so that their literary uses become merely illustrative of larger principles. In fact, the word Oedipus now makes us think of Freud, not of Sophocles. That is because psychoanalysis lays claim to an even greater antiquity: Oedipuses were living before Sophocles wrote about him, minds expressed their basic drives before artists seized upon them for subjects. Third, literature becomes something that psychoanalysis fancies it must validate; literature cannot know what it is doing, and in spite of its verbality, cannot speak for itself. It can only offer the practice for which Freud would provide the theory. Fourth, literature, by reason of being without theoretical comprehension of its own processes, uses words in an unconsidered way: it talks of love, when it might be better advised to speak of libido; it speaks of what Byron calls 'the gentlemanly vice of avarice' when it might better talk of anal erotism. So its putative revelations are imprecise. Finally, in the nineteenth century we looked to literature, especially to the novel, for news of the human mind; now we turn to psychoanalysis for the news behind the news.

Freud himself was at once respectful and disrespectful of literature. He acknowledged and even insisted that many of his discoveries about the psyche had been anticipated by literary works. In his discussion of Jensen's *Gradiva*, for example, he praised Jensen for just such an anticipation. Jensen, then still alive, was singularly ungratified by such a view of his work. But when Freud considered art at large, he was often (though not always) less laudatory. The writer sublimates his desires, or, as Freud says, 'the writer softens the egotistical character of his egoistic day-dream by altering and disguising it'.[1] Writing becomes a pleasurable cover-up, furtive rather than open, a repression of reality at least as much as it is an expression of it. It conceals neurosis rather than freeing from it. Qualities that writers have cherished, their aesthetic power, their inspiration and exaltation, their development of previously established forms, have no psychoanalytic standing; they are demystified, or it may be, explained away as results of more basic drives and appetites. Writers fancied they were eagles, and are only clams.

Sensing a challenge, the literary community responded uneasily to the new psychology, especially in an area where it is particularly intrusive, that of biography. Traditional biography has relied upon two kinds of information: documents such as letters, and written or oral reminiscences. These being absent, biographers have often made their surmises or conjectures on the basis of written works. Shakespeare, they think, was a bit like Hamlet as a young man and like Prospero as an old one, and books have been written on such speculations. Freud himself was not inhibited by scarcity of documents or oral histories. In an example mentioned by Dr Storr, Freud took up a reminiscence of Leonardo da Vinci of being in his cradle as an infant when a kite came and struck his mouth with its tail feathers. Freud insists that this was not a memory but a dream, he mistranslates kite as vulture, and on these beginnings offers a psychological sketch which takes in not only Leonardo's childhood but his mature paintings. In the same way, he finds Dostoevsky's parricidal guilt feelings to be the cause of that writer's immediately subsequent contraction of epilepsy. It appears, however, that the epilepsy did not develop until long afterwards. Freud is equally bold with a childhood memory of Goethe, of throwing crockery out of the window.[2] This he traces to the birth of a sibling, and does so quite plausibly, though we don't know whether the crockery was actually thrown at the time of a birth or not. No recent biographer has, I believe, followed Freud's theories of Leonardo, Dostoevsky, or Goethe. But Freud was perhaps just exploring possibilities. He was more resolute about his theory of Moses, though even here he worried that he 'was obliged to construct so imposing a statue upon

[1] *SE*, 9.153.

[2] 'A childhood recollection from *Dichtung und Wahrheit*', *SE*, 17.147-56.

feet of clay, so that any fool could topple it'.[3] He was perhaps more interested in the general truth of such psychological patterns than in their accuracy in the particular instance.

Jean-Paul Sartre wrote three huge volumes on Flaubert which take off from a similarly minuscule beginning. Flaubert's niece, Mme Caroline Commanville, wrote in old age about her uncle, and recalled his having confided that he could not learn to read at the age of nine. Unfortunately, we have a letter of Flaubert written just at the beginning of his ninth year, and written very well, in which he speaks of having already written plays. Sartre might have decided that Mme Commanville, writing as an old woman, had confused her uncle with somebody else. But he wants to use her reminiscence, so he decides that she has just made a little slip, and remembered that Flaubert said nine when he must have said seven. He then postulates that someone said to the boy of seven, who could not learn his letters, 'you are the idiot of the family'. (Those familiar with Sartre's writings will recall that in his biography of Genet he imagines that someone said to the child Genet, 'you are a thief'.) So the title of Sartre's biography of Flaubert is *The Idiot of the Family.*[4] Were we to object that the child Flaubert, even supposing that he had trouble learning to read, was in other ways precocious, I cannot imagine Sartre retreating. For ultimately Flaubert must be shown to fail in the eyes of his family, and I think we could say, in the eyes of Sartre. And if Sartre lacked the testimony of Mme Commanville, however unreliable that testimony may be, he is quite willing to say that by observing the effects in the mature Flaubert, we can reason back to the causes in Flaubert the child. Given a particular kind of dog's tail, we can deduce a particular kind of muzzle.

The rigorous scrutiny which psychoanalysis offers writers, depriving them of their élite status and sitting as a sort of posthumous authority to take note of their aberrations and concealments, has roused considerable misgivings among them. There has been no one response to Freud. Thomas Mann belauded him, as Professor Lloyd-Jones points out. Auden begins the Prologue to *The Orators*, 'By landscape reminded once of his mother's figure,' and we realize

[3] Letter from Freud to Arnold Zweig, 16 December 1934, in *The Letters of Sigmund Freud and Arnold Zweig*, ed. Ernst L. Freud, translated by W.D. Robson-Scott and Mrs Robson-Scott (London, 1970), p.98.

[4] *L'Idiot de la famille*, 3 vols (Paris, 1971-2).

we are in the age of Freud. T.S. Eliot's reaction was more mixed: in 'The Dry Salvages' he said that 'to explore the womb, or tomb, or dreams is among the usual / Pastimes and drugs, and features of the press,' though in *The Cocktail Party* he included among the characters a benign and unworldly psychoanalyst. Joyce in *Finnegans Wake* speaks mockingly of the time 'when we were jung and easily freudened,' but he was perhaps the first writer to use Freudian slips in a conscious way. Leopold Bloom speaks of 'the wife's admirers' when he consciously means 'the wife's advisers' and unconsciously thinks of his own wife's admirer; and his tongue slips again when he speaks of that admirer as his wife's 'business menagerer' instead of 'business manager'. Joyce did not subscribe to the Freud-Jones theory of *Hamlet* as Oedipal conflict, though it fascinated him, and in *Ulysses* he centred a psychological explanation of the play in the feelings of the dead king rather than of the living son, *Hamlet* without the prince almost. Joyce turned down a suggestion that he be analysed by Jung, but he allowed Jung to attempt to cure his distraught daughter. In a later generation Ernest Hemingway would revolt against the idea that his works were the result of a psychic trauma rather than of the utmost aesthetic cunning. There are of course examples of writers who have been analysed, such as H.D. and Doris Lessing, but other writers have felt that the peculiar synthesis of weakness and strength which constituted their gift would not profit by being anatomized. Erich Fromm advised Conrad Aiken not to risk it.

Of course, writers have always been dubious about putting their lives at the mercy of biographers. They could see that they had much to lose, and probably little to gain, by having their pasts reconstructed without the right of reply. Oscar Wilde remarked that biography 'adds to death a new terror, and makes one wish that all art were anonymous'. Thomas Carlyle declared that 'the biographies of men of letters are for the most part the saddest chapter in the history of the human race except the Newgate Calendar'. For while traditional biography was usually animated by a desire to be adulatory or when necessary exculpatory, it could scarcely fail to present details which were irrelevant or perhaps at odds with this motive. The lives of creative writers, as of other men, cannot consist only of moments of victorious self-transcendence and transcendence of circumstances, but must include pettinesses and humiliations. Of this Freud was well aware. In 1936 Arnold Zweig offered to write his biography. Freud responded that he was too fond of Zweig to permit it. 'To be a biographer,' he said, 'you must tie yourself up in lies, concealments, hypocrisies, false colourings, and even in hiding a lack of understanding, for biographical truth is not to be had, and if it were to be had, we could not use it.' He went on, 'truth is not feasible, mankind doesn't deserve it, and anyway isn't our prince Hamlet right when he says that if we all had our deserts, which of us would 'scape whipping?'[5] So he offers two objections, somewhat self-contradictory: one that biographers tell lies, the other that if they told truths the truths would be unbearable. He found a discreet biographer in Ernest Jones, who skirted many of those issues that Freud would have dealt with in other men, and, though a psychoanalyst, made no effort at psychoanalysis.

Given such cogent objections, even from Freud himself, to biographical undertakings, the proliferation of biography in our century is astonishing. The advance tremors that dying writers have felt have proved justified. Scarcely has their breath left them when their widows or widowers feel obliged to choose among the outstretched pens of eager memorializers. There is hardly time for mourning; the public's appetite for information must be filled as soon as the grave. This appetite is not altogether discreditable. We long to understand our world, and imagine we can do so by understanding the vivid personalities within it. We want to bring them back to life, so far as we can. With literary men this impulse is especially understandable, for while television figures – politicians or athletes or newscasters – are people we can recognize like old acquaintances, writers work in such strict privacy and are generally so secretive about their intentions and sources that we look at their lives with even keener interest. We wish that the biographer would explain the mainsprings of genius. Freud acknowledged that the comprehension of genius was beyond his powers, and later biographers, without disclaiming the task, have had less success at it than we hoped.

No doubt we have also, in reading or writing biography, a less noble aim, a gossipy one, to confirm through the details of a life that a gifted man or woman, though in many ways unlike us, is, like us

[5] Freud to Zweig, 31 May 1936, *Letters*, p.127. I have slightly retouched the translation.

too, subject to the same needs, smelling equally of mortality. We at once want them to present themselves on the same stage that we occupy, and yet – for we have not given up the heroic altogether – we want them undiminished.

Freud understood that his own case histories were close to biographies; he called them pathographies. Yet health and disease are so intermingled by his theory that no one can escape being a potential patient. The universality of the pathic is one of his discoveries, as Dr Rycroft complains. His epoch seems based on the aphorism: one touch of kinkiness makes the whole world kin. Normality, healthy sexuality, and similar terms are out of order. The ordinary is as subject to scrutiny as the extraordinary. Freud's case histories are however biographies without heroes, as they are without villains. They are also biographies without history, for the linear past interests him less than the imaginative past, especially the mythology of childhood which may well be partially invented by the patient to suit his later needs, and which may suddenly obtrude itself quite out of regular order. There is no time in the unconscious, as Freud points out. Whether we saw the primal scene or not, he eventually decided, was irrelevant; we thought we did, we imagined we did, and that is enough. We live among feelings, to which facts may or may not adhere. Biographers have never felt so free of the necessity of distinguishing fact from fantasy.

Towards biography as practised before his time Freud was severe. He regarded it as based on deliberate concealment. In his essay on Leonardo he said that the majority of biographers pass over in silence the subject's sexual activity or sexual individuality, and therefore cannot arrive at an understanding of the subject's mental life. On this point he was obviously right. Pre-Freudian biographers were averse to breaking taboos about sexual details. Froude had heard from a close friend of Jane Carlyle, on her deathbed, that Carlyle was impotent; but in four long volumes of biography of Carlyle he avoids mention of this point. While novelists, especially in France, were becoming increasingly open about sexuality, biographers were slow to follow, and tended to cling to notions of respectability that novelists were trying to dislodge.

Freud also declared that 'biographers are fixated on their heroes in a quite special way. In many cases,' he says,

> they have chosen their hero as the subject of their studies because – for reasons of their personal emotional life – they have felt a special affection for him from the very first. They then devote their energies to a task of idealization, aimed at enrolling the great man among the class of their infant models – at reviving in him, perhaps, the child's idea of his father. To gratify this wish they obliterate the individual features of their subject's physiognomy. They smooth over the traces of his life's struggle with internal and external resistances, and they tolerate in him no vestige of human weakness or imperfection. They thus present us with what is in fact a cold, strange, ideal figure, instead of a human being to whom we might feel ourselves distantly related. That they should do this is regrettable, for they thereby sacrifice truth to an illusion, and for the sake of their infantile phantasies abandon the opportunity of penetrating the most fascinating secrets of human nature.[6]

This is a vehement indictment that Freud makes, though now a little out of date. I should doubt that modern biographers are fixated on their subjects or look in them for father figures (or even mother figures, a possibility that Freud characteristically ignored). The modern biographer has read Freud, or even if he has not, he has absorbed him. He has come to recognize the dangers of fixation and idealization. The biography of Woodrow Wilson that Freud purportedly wrote with William C. Bullitt originated in what might be called counter-fixation, in active dislike, as they admit. If a modern biographer identifies himself a little with his subject, he does so reservedly, and withdraws a bit at the same time.

And it must be said that the subject of the literary biographer – the writer – has also become more wary, apprehensive of being psychoanalysed too easily. An analyst of my acquaintance tells me that he rarely sees among educated people in cities the classic symptoms of hysteria, such as paralysis of an arm or leg, inability to speak or swallow, fainting or convulsions, which were so marked when Freud began to delineate hysteria. Even hysterics know a cliché. But an Austrian analyst tells me, 'in Vienna we have still the classic symptoms'. Now that our possession of an Oedipus complex has been dinned into us from our early years, writers are much less prone to present so acknowledged a behaviour pattern. Were Sophocles alive today, he would write about someone else than

[6] *SE*, 11.130.

Oedipus. Other discoveries of Freud, such as meaningful slips of the tongue, are grasped at once by the tongue-slipper, not to mention by his auditors, and so seem to bear a reduced significance, as if whatever was being repressed was not repressed very far down. If we have an accident, we know all about accident proneness, though this may not stop the pain. Nor do we fall so easily into the error marked out by Freud of being too hero-oriented. The unheroic interests us too – moments of shabby conduct, or symptoms of disease – Freud's own jaw cancer for example. Biographers are often accused of indecorum, and reply by accusing their detractors of squeamishness.

Our conception of the creative process has undergone such an upheaval that we no longer look, as a nineteenth-century biographer would, for evidence of the taking of infinite pains that genius traditionally is said to constitute. Mere gumption does not impress us. In the last century it was assumed that literary works came into being because their authors willed them to. The modern biographer would question the autonomy of that will. He would be likely to see the writer as the victim of internal compulsions, or familial and extra-familial complications, bursting into literature willy-nilly, writing not to express finesses but, it may be, to exorcize horrors. Henri Michaux, in one of his imaginary voyages, describes how a people whom he calls Les Hacs rear their artists. It might be a parable of our present conception:

> The Hacs have arranged to rear every year a few child martyrs, whom they subject to harsh treatment and evident injustices, inventing reasons and deceptive complications, based on lies, for everything, in an atmosphere of terror and mystery.
>
> Entrusted with this work are some hardhearted men, real brutes, directed by cruel and clever overseers.
>
> In this way they have reared up great artists, great poets, but also, unfortunately, assassins and especially reformers – incredible bitterenders.
>
> If a change is made in the customs and social institutions, it's owing to them; if, in spite of their small army, the Hacs have nothing to fear, again they owe it to them; if, in their straightforward language, lightning flashes of anger have been fixed, beside which the honeyed deviousness of foreign writers seems insipid dog food, it is again to them they owe it, to a few ragged, wretched, hopeless kids.[7]

[7] *Selected Writings*, translated by Richard Ellmann (New York, 1968), pp.140-1.

Art, by these lights, is not the result of virtue but of handicap. Matthew Arnold admired Sophocles for seeing life steadily and seeing it whole. We on the other hand admire our writers because they respond with fury and passion to abuse and indignity. The wise contemplative visage of Goethe is not our model, but the hurt, furtive face of Kafka. When Joyce in *Ulysses* has Stephen Dedalus offer us a portrait of Shakespeare, it is not the swan of Avon serenely regarding the human scene, but a vengeful cuckold writing out of anger and jealousy. I think we can attribute to Freud the way that our biographical attention has been directed away from the perfection of artifacts and onto the imperfection of artificers. Yeats reminds us that all the artistic ladders start in the foul rag and boneshop of the heart, and the rag and boneshop is what we want to examine – not the empyrean loft to which the ladders go. So Robert Lowell, an imperfect poet, wrote in a late poem that imperfection is the language of art. Sartre conceives of Flaubert as saying to himself, 'loser wins,' as if only through defeat in life is victory in art possible. The writer gets his own back by writing.

If we try to isolate the features of modern biography, the first is its heightened sensitivity. I think we can attribute this in large part to Freud. The biographer conceives of himself not as outside but as inside the subject's mind, not as observing but as ferreting. Facts do not speak for themselves. We model ourselves on Freud, analysts without couches. What Freud instructs us, as Philip Rieff observes, is to recognize all experience as symptomatic. Trivia have as much to tell us as crises. We should all like to collect tell-tale slips of tongue or pen, for example, although these are not so easy to find as perhaps *The Psychopathology of Everyday Life* makes them seem. We live in what Paul Ricoeur in his book on Freud calls the age of suspicion; we do not so much present as arraign. Sartre, in writing of Baudelaire as in writing of Flaubert, often seems the prosecuting attorney, when an earlier biographer would have been attorney for the defence.

The conviction that everything is relevant is somewhat destructive of chronology. The nineteenth century could view a life as a progress from primitive childhood to civilized adulthood, followed perhaps by the return to primitivism in dotage. But Freud makes us recognize that linear development may not describe the psyche adequately, that *Nachträglichkeit* or deferred action may suddenly project the being into new areas, as hitherto suppressed parts of the self manifest themselves.[8] The ahistorical unconscious is constantly obtruding into the historical layers of the mind. Moreover, the unity of the self is likely to be relinquished by the biographer in favour of a more protean entity. Like the wizened Christ child in some early Italian paintings, we are born old. Sexualized from birth, ridden by undirected or half-directed fantasies, we have no time to grow up even if we have the will. Sartre suggests that a life is simply a childhood with the stops pulled out; but it might well be a childhood with many of the stops pushed in even further. Our seeming selves are only palimpsests under which may be dimly perceived features successfully or unsuccessfully repressed. If we persist in regarding the self as in some sense one rather than many, we have still to allow for what Sartre calls its carousel of motives moving about the pool of its central ipseity.

The lesson that Freud inculcates, of our sexual nature, has been learned almost too well. The word Freudian has become a synonym for sexual, although Freud makes clear in his essay, '"Wild" psycho-analysis',[9] how wrong this is, because repression is an essential part of sexuality. The nineteenth-century reticence of which he complained is hard to discover in our contemporary behaviour. We are quite prepared to make our sometimes naive deductions from what we can find out about bedroom quirks. That Ruskin's moral fervour derived in large part from his sexual fears, and that Carlyle's pungency compensated for sexual impotence, are near commonplaces of biographical interpretation. The latest biographies of Fitzgerald and Auden not only discuss their mating habits but their genital sizes. We are all prepared to acknowledge what Freud called somatic compliance, the body's submission to the mind, as well as its opposite, the mind's submission to the body. Even Yeats says, 'our bodies are nearer ... to the "unconscious" than our thoughts'.[10] On the other hand, when Sartre says that Flaubert's maternal grandfather, after the death of his wife in childbirth, took revenge upon the new-born infant by sickening and then dying himself, we become sceptical, especially when we discover that his death did not occur until ten years later. What protracted vindictiveness!

[8] *SE*, 4.205.
[9] *SE*, 11.219-30.
[10] *Explorations* (London, 1962), pp.446-7.

Psychoanalysis may also relieve our envy of sexual athletes; their success may be as pathological as the commoner unsuccess. Don Giovanni is not sensual, he is sick; he needs a hospital, not a hell. Maybe.

The effect of our new-found methods of detection is vast and unpredictable. The unknown need not be the unknowable. To paraphrase Freud, where obscurity was, hypothesis shall be. In this sense, paucity of information may even be an advantage, as freeing the mind for conjecture. The early years, to which psychoanalysis attaches so much importance, are just those about which we know least. But there are mysteries throughout. Where direct evidence is missing, we have to rely on outside testimony. The witness of friends or relatives may or may not be helpful. A recent collection of taped interviews with friends of Wallace Stevens[11] is proof of how little his friends knew him. Of course, there are always letters. The modern biographer is aware that the letter is itself a literary form, through which writer and recipient play a game of concealment and revealment. What we have to read in correspondence is what is not written there, as at a party we notice who has not been invited. For earlier biographers, letters were saints' relics; for biographers since Freud, they are likely to be duplicitous or at least incomplete.

In presenting his subject a biographer agrees with Freud that we must be sceptical of heroics. We have always known, even without Freud's help, or Rochefoucauld's, that our virtues are often vices in disguise. Now the existence of virtue is itself almost in question. In Eliot's *Murder in the Cathedral* the last temptation of Thomas à Becket is that of martyrdom. We cannot even die for a cause without worrying that it may be just a means of self-aggrandizement. Self-sacrifice is another virtue that has lost much of its earlier prestige. Oscar Wilde connected it with the self-mutilation of savages. The appetite for suffering is one of which Freud has made us intensely conscious. The concept of sadomasochism has put to flight many seemingly virtuous acts. For what Freud tells us, though he never said so explicitly, is that the stomach hunts the ulcer.

Just as virtues have taken on a little viciousness, so vices have lost some of theirs. The vice of extravagance is such a failing.

[11] Peter Brazeau, *Parts of a World: Wallace Stevens Remembered, An Oral Biography* (New York, 1983).

Questionable as a method of household economy, it may be defensible when applied to literary innovation. Joyce regarded himself as guilty of both kinds. Drunkenness may be reprehensible in itself, but as a control over schizophrenia, as Jung said Joyce used it, it may have its merits. Abysses of shyness and evasion may underlie dogmatism, inner firmness may be concealed under wobbling and waffling. Lautréamont said of his fearful book *Les Chants de Maldoror* that he had indeed, like Byron, Baudelaire, and others, sung the praises of evil. 'Of course I exaggerated a bit in order to make an original contribution to the kind of sublime literature that only sings of despair in order to depress the reader and make him long for goodness as a remedy.'[12] Beckett's work proceeds somewhat differently; it undercuts despair by saving humour, and undercuts saving humour by unsalvagable despair. All that is certain is uncertainty. Contradictory impulses may coincide; as Freud tells us, there is no *no* in the unconscious. Lacan points out, 'what the unconscious forces us to examine is the law according to which no utterance can ever be reduced simply to its own statement'.[13] When Yeats asks whether he believes in that farrago of occultism and philosophy and poetry which he calls *A Vision*, he seems to reply that he both does and does not, and that the question of belief may not belong to our age, and that truth can be embodied in a poet's life but not known. George Eliot, in a sentence admired by Henry James, spoke of 'the suppressed transitions which unite all contrasts'. Freud's term, reaction-formation, indicates how we may repress a wish by doing the exact opposite of it. The modern biographer recognizes that every motive is a multiplicity of motives, many of them in conflict; as Michaux says, we are born of too many others.

We must infer that biography has plunged into a new phase. At the same time, many biographies are not written in full awareness of what has been happening. The responsibilities of this kind of subtle and devious interpretation are so manifold that few practitioners rush to take them all on. Their failure to do so is not reprehensible. For one thing, the information they have about matters which are crucial for Freud is often scanty, and they may be reluctant,

[12] Alex de Jonge, *Nightmare Culture: Lautréamont and 'Les Chants de Maldoror'* (London, 1973), p.19.

[13] Jacques Lacan, *Ecrits* (Paris, 1966), p.892.

understandably, to introduce their own speculations as if they commanded equal attention with known particulars. Another is that the tracing of ultimate causes may reduce differentiation: the biographies of Woodrow Wilson by Freud and Bullitt, of Martin Luther by Erikson, and of Flaubert by Sartre, all make so much of their Oedipal complexes and their relation to God the Father, that the president, the religious reformer, and the writer might almost be confused with one another. The unconscious is a great melting pot. Even Freud sometimes apologizes for the repetitiveness of certain psychological patterns, and a biographer who depends heavily upon them is likely to create a stereotype instead of a person.

It seems probable that certain patterns made available by psychoanalysis may have a blurring effect. For example, among the character traits isolated by Freud is the anal erotic. Edmund Wilson attributed this quality to Ben Jonson. It could as easily be attributed to Ernest Hemingway. For Hemingway, unlike his prodigal friend Fitzgerald, was always gathering, absorbing, hoarding, withholding. He prided himself on his secrets, and his method of writing was to offer information as sparingly as possible. 'You'll lose it if you talk about it,' says Jake in *Fiesta*. For Hemingway writing was a kind of suppression with only partial release. He behaved in life as in his art, going without food to save money, then engaging in some gush of expense, but all the time keeping a money heap in reserve. His capacity for retention extended to keeping his early notebooks in bank vaults for many years, for future exploitation. Even his method of composing a paragraph in circles around key words suggests a peristaltic movement. Though he wanted to be known as swashbuckling, his strength came from self-concealment. His well-known competitiveness was as much as anything an attempt to protect his winter stores.

A biographer of Hemingway will certainly wish to present this character trait. But the fact that it was presumably shared by Ben Jonson – so different a writer – may make us less cocky about what we have found. Could it be that anal erotism is pretty general among writers? They are usually inclined to be thrifty, to build up reserve supplies, to play ant rather than grasshopper. Whether there is any physical parallel – whether their bowels behave anally erotically – we can rarely find out. But one thing is sure: the daring innovation in style of Hemingway, its fanatical economy, like the humour and lyricism of Ben Jonson, may be disparaged by offering it in the context of anal erotism.

Another post-Freudian situation arises in biography when the biographer shapes, to the point of distortion, the facts at his disposal in accordance with Freudian theory. Henry James, as is well-known and confirmed by love letters to a man, was predominantly homosexual. Freud offers several explanations of homosexuality, including a genetic one, but the one he expounds most prominently, as in his essay on Leonardo da Vinci, is that the homosexual is fixated on the mother. (Freud regretted later that he had had so little to go on in this essay.) In Leon Edel's biography of James, Edel searches for evidence that James's mother 'smothered' her son Henry. Unfortunately the evidence is lacking, and almost all the testimony he gives – from friends, relatives, or Henry James himself – appears to differ with this conclusion. Of course, one can still say that it is true without evidence. In an area where witnesses are so hard to come by, speculation can be rife. An aphorism of our time for Freudian biography might be: if you can't see it, it must be there. Still, caution is necessary if we would persuade others.

It has required the assurance of Jean-Paul Sartre to carry out a full-scale biography of the modern kind. Though not by any means an orthodox Freudian, since he finds the unconscious to be conscious, he still keeps largely to Freudian patterns. He has little to say of the feat of Flaubert in remaking the novel, partly because he is suspicious of literature; in particular, Sartre is contemptuous of late nineteenth-century literature, which he calls an 'art-neurosis' engineered by the Knights of Nothingness, whose ideals he finds to be anti-human. Flaubert was a Knight of Nothingness, and Sartre's interest is in showing how he came to be one. I have already mentioned the slender memories to which he often attaches so much weight. When questioned as to how he knows something about Flaubert, he has the assurance to reply, 'well, I've read Flaubert'. And though he insists that life and work should not be equated, he does equate them again and again. For example, he relies heavily upon patterns he claims to find in Flaubert's early stories. When he has to allow that these stories are common ones of the period, very much to hand for Flaubert, he counters by asking why Flaubert – faced with many common stories – picked these particular ones.

The argument is conducted with great force and wit. Still, it is not quite so convincing as he imagines. In the stories, for example, he is particularly eager to find instances of sibling rivalries. Usually in the stories the older brother is triumphant, thus confirming Sartre's conjecture that Flaubert felt victimized by his elder brother. But in one story the younger brother is triumphant. Sartre is not fazed: he announces that this time Flaubert has 'shuffled the cards'. But of course, the question arises, why did he not shuffle the cards some more? And if shuffling the cards is to be conceded, then how do we know that the other stories, in which the older brother is triumphant, are not the ones which have been shuffled the most? I think that we know enough about the creative process to insist that the erect pen has no conscience, that Flaubert may well have imported details from other lives rather than from his own, or just tried his hand at a story which he had happened to hear or read recently. There is always the hopeful possibility, which occurs to the reader as Sartre completes his accusatory case against his subject, that Flaubert's family life was quite different from the nightmare version Sartre conjures up. Sartre offers Flaubert no liberty, keeps him on a tight leash, binds him hand and foot, fetish and phobia. With certain presuppositions about family life, largely based on Freud, Sartre can prove his case over and over again. His eloquence about the unknown is staggering. The flimsier the documentation, the more he has to say. When facts are mentioned, they come as a relief. Substitutions are everywhere: about one of Flaubert's stories Sartre insists that the father is really the mother, and the mother the father. (Later on he says that Flaubert's father mothered him after his breakdown at Pont-L'Evêque.) He has also the family romance at its most intense: not only does son murder father but father murders son. This is grand stuff, and we wish it could be confirmed.

I think that Sartre indicates the merits and demerits of modern biographical method. On the one hand, thanks to Freud, we have been alerted to all sorts of complexities in the personality. On the other hand, these can be interpreted so variously that it is hard to establish firm footing. Where everything can stand for its opposite, where fantasies and facts intertwine, we look desperately for a position in time and space. Freud is supposed to have said that there are times when a cigar is just a cigar. But how to recognize these tranquil moments of simple identity?

That Freud makes biography difficult does not mean that he

should be put aside. Biographers need a depth psychology, and Freud, with his followers and deviationists, offers one. Conceptualizing a life is different from living it; experiences cannot be simply transcribed onto paper without filtering them through an alien consciousness. Perhaps we should be gingerly in applying Freud's theories, for it is when they are most ostentatious that they awaken most uneasiness. Yet if Sartre runs too fast, not to run at all would be craven. A modern biographer is bound to attend to incursions of the irrational upon the rational, to look for unexpected connections and unsuspected motivations. For all this Freud remains a model, though no doubt a tricky one.

CHAPTER FOUR

The Symbol of the Veil: Psychological Reflections on Schiller's Poetry

E.H. Gombrich

Friedrich Schiller is not a household word among educated people in the English-speaking world, and I trust nobody will take it amiss if I mention that he was born in November 1759 ten years after Goethe, that unlike Goethe he had a harsh and rebellious youth, but earned an ever-increasing reputation first as professor of history at Jena, and then as playwright, moving to Weimar, where he died in May 1805. Needless to say, the stages and facets of this varied career had given rise to an enormous bibliography,[1] and have never been neglected by specialists in departments of German language and literature. But these signal achievements of Anglo-Saxon critics and historians, from which I have gratefully profited as much as circumstances permitted, stand in obvious contrast to the benevolent ignorance of the general public. When I asked for an edition of Schiller's poetry in two of the main academic bookshops of London, the helpful sales assistants were genuinely surprised, because they had never heard that Schiller had written any poetry. I know that this happened *in partibus infidelium* and that perhaps I would have had more luck in Oxford. The translations I have supplied lack all literary pretensions,

[1] *Schiller Bibliographie*, by Wolfgang Vulpius *et al.* (Berlin, 1959-). Where I found references useful for the identification of passages I have cited by volume and page number the edition of Schiller's *Sämtliche Werke*, ed. Gerhard Fricke and Herbert G. Göpfert (Munich, 1965), hereafter abbreviated as *SW*.

though I have occasionally allowed the lines to scan if this required no effort on my part.

Let me express the hope, though, that no one will judge the quality of Schiller's verse from this *ad hoc* selection and translation. I believe that the best of Schiller's philosophical poetry is quite unique in literature. Those who see in Schiller mainly the philosopher who applied the insights of Kant to the criticism of literature may be tempted to regard these poems as a late flowering of the didactic genre which goes back to Lucretius and flourished in the eighteenth century, say, in the poetry of Erasmus Darwin. But in claiming them to be unique I wanted to indicate that such a reading would be one-sided. Wilhelm von Humboldt, who was in constant intellectual contact with the poet at the time when he produced these masterpieces, and even occasionally suggested amendments in wording and versification, testified that Schiller's philosophical ideas developed out of the medium of his imagination and his feelings, adding that this was obvious in the case of a poet.[2] In other words the poetic vision came first in Schiller, and though he struggled manfully and successfully also to translate his visions into the systematic language of Kantian philosophy, his profound and difficult philosophical prose works can also be seen as attempts to rationalize and communicate his basic emotional concerns.

With this assertion I have taken up our theme of psychoanalysis and its influence on the arts and humanities. No doubt it is this influence which has made me use the term rationalization, and has prompted me to look at a recurrent image of Schiller's philosophical poems with more than purely rhetorical interest. But though this influence and this interest go far back in my intellectual life to the time when I collaborated with Ernst Kris on problems of the theory of art, this approach has never interfered with my admiration for Schiller's creation. There may be applications of psychoanalysis to art or poetry which incur this danger and indeed deserve the strictures of C.S. Lewis in his witty essay on 'Psycho-analysis and literary criticism'.[3] But luckily we have the words of Freud himself

[2] Humboldt's *Vorerinnerung über Schiller und den Gang seiner Geistesentwicklung* (1830) with which he prefaced his edition of their correspondence, *Der Briefwechsel zwischen Friedrich Schiller und Wilhelm von Humboldt*, ed. Siegfried Seidel (Berlin, 1962).

[3] Reprinted in *They asked for a Paper* (London, 1962), pp.120-38.

to guard against this type of reductionism. Writing about his paper on Dostoevsky to Stefan Zweig in 1920, Freud explained that, 'with you I need not fear the misunderstanding that any emphasis on the so-called pathological elements aims at minimizing or explaining the magnificence of Dostoevski's poetic creativity'.[4] I certainly wish neither to minimize nor to explain the magnificence of the poetic creativity of Friedrich Schiller. What I have learned from psychoanalysis is rather to respect the ability of the genius to transmute the impulses arising from emotional conflicts into valid creations, valid not only for him but also for others. I have neither the competence, nor, to be frank, much confidence in the use of the technical terminology in which psychoanalysis describes this process of transformation. But I am not sure that it will be needed here in any case, when discussing the work of an exceptional poet and thinker. Freud himself sometimes expressed the conviction that writers and poets have an intuitive insight into the secret workings of their own and other men's minds which anticipated and matched the more systematic accounts of his theory. In other words they were conscious of many things which are often located in the Freudian unconscious. Strangely enough Friedrich Schiller was here more popish than the pope or more Freudian than Freud. In a remarkable letter to Goethe of 27 March 1801 he comes to speak of the role of the unconscious in art and poetry – though he calls it not *das Unbewusste* but *das Bewusstlose*, the lack in consciousness. He was taking issue with the Romantic philosophy of Schelling, who had maintained that Nature started from the unconscious in order to raise it to consciousness while art started from the conscious and ended in the unconscious – a discussion, by the way, which may remind you of the many links between psychoanalysis and German Romanticism. In any case Schiller retorted that experience shows that the poet also starts exclusively from the unconscious; indeed he can consider himself lucky if, by means of the clearest consciousness of what he is doing, he can get so far that he can again recognize his first dark global idea of his work undiminished in the finished process. 'Without such a dark but powerful global idea,' he continues, 'which precedes all technical elaboration, no work of poetry can come into being.' 'Poetry,' he suggests, 'consists precisely in the ability to

[4] Freud, *Briefe, 1873-1939*, ed. Ernst L. Freud (Frankfurt am Main, 1960), p.332.

express and communicate that unconscious, and to translate it into an object' – we might say to objectify it. What makes the poet, Schiller concludes, is the ability to unite the unconscious with awareness ('das Bewusstlose mit dem Besonnenen vereinigt macht den poetischen Künstler aus').[5]

I hope this formulation from Schiller's own hand empowers me now to go in search of the total idea, the global idea, which he has objectivized in so many of his works. As I have indicated in my title I find it embodied in an image or metaphor which frequently recurs in his *oeuvre*, the image of the veil. Let me then start from the poem of 1795 which centres on this very image or emblem, 'Das verschleierte Bild von Sais' ('The veiled image of Sais'), which takes us to the legendary sages of ancient Egypt, the priests of the Temple of Isis who also figure in Mozart's *Magic Flute*, which was then triumphing in the opera houses of Europe after the composer's premature death.

An eager youth had gone to the sanctuary in search of initiation, explaining to his guide that, truth being undivided, he wants nothing but the whole truth.

Indem sie einst so sprachen, standen sie
In einer einsamen Rotonde still,
Wo ein verschleiert Bild von Riesengrösse
Dem Jüngling in die Augen fiel. Verwundert
Blickt er den Führer an und spricht: 'Was ist's,
Das hinter diesem Schleier sich verbirgt?' –
'Die Wahrheit', ist die Antwort – 'Wie?' ruft jener,
'Nach Wahrheit streb ich ja allein, und diese
Gerade ist es, die man mir verhüllt?'

'Das mache mit der Gottheit aus', versetzt
Der Hierophant. 'Kein Sterblicher, sagt sie,
Rückt diesen Schleier, bis ich selbst ihn hebe.
Und wer mit ungeweihter, schuld'ger Hand
Den heiligen, verbotnen früher hebt,
Der, spricht die Gottheit' – 'Nun?' 'Der sieht die Wahrheit.'
'Ein seltsamer Orakelspruch! Du selbst,
Du hättest also niemals ihn gehoben?'
'Ich? Wahrlich nicht! Und war auch nie dazu

[5] I have throughout translated from the edition, *Schillers Briefe*, ed. Fritz Jonas (Stuttgart [1892-1922]).

Versucht' – 'Das fass ich nicht. Wenn von der Wahrheit
Nur diese dünne Scheidewand mich trennte' –
'Und ein Gezetz', fällt ihm sein Führer ein,
'Gewichtiger, mein Sohn, als du es meinst,
Ist dieser dünne Flor – Für deine Hand
Zwar leicht, doch zentnerschwer für dein Gewissen.'

Der Jüngling ging gedankenvoll nach Hause;
Ihm raubt des Wissens brennende Begier
Den Schlaf, er wälzt sich glühend auf dem Lager
Und rafft sich auf um Mitternacht. Zum Tempel
Führt unfreiwillig ihn der scheue Tritt.
Leicht ward es ihm, die Mauer zu ersteigen,
Und mitten in das Innre der Rotonde
Trägt ein beherzter Sprung den Wagenden.

Hier steht er nun, und grauenvoll umfängt
Den Einsamen die lebenlose Stille,
Die nur der Tritte hohler Widerhall
In den geheimen Grüften unterbricht.
Von oben durch der Kuppel Öffnung wirft
Der Mond den bleichen, silberblauen Schein,
Und furchtbar wie ein gegenwärt'ger Gott
Erglänzt durch des Gewölbes Finsternisse
In ihrem langen Schleier die Gestalt.

Er tritt hinan mit ungewissem Schritt;
Schon will die freche Hand das Heilige berühren,
Da zuckt es heiss und kühl durch sein Gebein,
Und stösst ihn weg mit unsichtbarem Arme.
Unglücklicher, was willst du tun? So ruft
In seinem Innern eine treue Stimme.
Versuchen den Allheiligen willst du?
Kein Sterblicher, sprach des Orakels Mund,
Rückt diesen Schleier, bis ich selbst ihn hebe.
Doch setzte nicht derselbe Mund hinzu:
Wer diesen Schleier hebt, soll Wahrheit schauen?
'Sei hinter ihm, was will! Ich heb ihn auf.'
(Er ruft's mit lauter Stimm.) 'Ich will sie schauen.' 'Schauen'!
Gellt ihm ein langes Echo spottend nach.

Er spricht's und hat den Schleier aufgedeckt.
'Nun,' fragt ihr, 'und was zeigte sich ihm hier?'
Ich weiss es nicht. Besinnungslos und bleich,
So fanden ihn am andern Tag die Priester
Am Fussgestell der Isis ausgestreckt.
Was er allda gesehen und erfahren,
Hat seine Zunge nie bekannt. Auf ewig
War seines Lebens Heiterkeit dahin,
Ihn riss ein tiefer Gram zum frühen Grabe.
'Weh Dem', dies war sein warnungsvolles Wort,
Wenn ungestüme Frager in ihn drangen,
'Weh Dem, der zu der Wahrheit geht durch Schuld,
Sie wird ihm nimmermehr erfreulich sein.'

While they were talking in this vein they found themselves
In the interior of a lone rotunda
Where a veiled image of gigantic size
Impressed the youth, who, with a sense of wonder,
Looked at his guide and asked him, 'What is this
That hides behind this veil?' – 'Truth', was the answer.
'What?' he exclaims, 'it's after Truth alone I strive
And now Truth is to be concealed from me?'

'That you must settle with the Goddess', said
The hierophant. 'No mortal hand', said she,
'May lift this veil till I myself shall lift it.
But he whose sacrilegious guilty hand
Will grasp at this forbidden sacred veil,
He' – says the Goddess – 'Well?' – 'will look on Truth.'
– 'What strange oracular words, and you yourself
Have never lifted it?'
'I? Surely not, nor did I ever feel such a temptation.'
'I cannot grasp this – if Truth and I
Were separated by this thin division' –
'And by a law', said rapidly the guide,
'This flimsy veil weighs little in your hand,
But on your conscience it weighs hundredweights'.

The youth went home by many thoughts oppressed.
His thirst for knowledge robbed him of his sleep
And restlessly he tossed upon his bed.
When midnight came he rose, and to the temple
Involuntarily he turned his steps.

To scale the wall was easy and a leap
Took the bold youth inside the sanctuary
Where soon he came to the rotunda's centre.

So there he stands, and with a sense of dread
The lifeless stillness grips the lonely youth.
Only the hollow echo of his steps,
Reverberates from the mysterious vault,
While from the opening of the dome above
The moonlight pours its pale and silvery blue.
And fearful, like the presence of a God,
A shining apparition in the gloom,
In its enormous veil the statue stands.

So, moving closer with unsteady steps,
His ruthless hand is reaching for the Holy
When heat and cold run through his bones and marrow
And hold him off with an invisible arm.
Unfortunate, what deed is this? So calls
A faithful voice within his inner self.
Are you to tempt the Holiest of Holies?
No mortal, said the Oracle, you know,
Must move this veil, till I move it myself.
But did these self-same lips not also say
That he who lifts it will behold the Truth?
'Be what it may behind, I lift it now.'
(He calls in a loud voice.) 'I want to see her.'
'See her,' a strident echo mockingly repeats.

So said, he seized the cover of the veil.
'Well', you will ask, 'what was it that he saw?'
I cannot tell; unconscious, pale and wan
The temple priests discovered him next morning
Prostrate before the pedestal of Isis.
Whatever there he saw and there experienced
Did never pass his lips, for evermore
All cheerfulness had vanished from his life.
A searing grief soon brought him to his grave.
'O woe to him' – these were his warning words
When he was importuned by questioners.
'O woe to him who comes to Truth through guilt,
For it will never, never, bring him joy.'

We can guess where Schiller found the legend which so inspired him. It must have been in the footnote which Immanuel Kant appended to a paragraph of his *Critique of Judgement* which deals with genius:

> Perhaps there has never been a more sublime utterance, or a thought more sublimely expressed, than the well-known inscription upon the Temple of *Isis* (Mother Nature): 'I am all that is, and that was, and that shall be, and no mortal hath raised the veil from before my face'.

Kant continues by commending a book on 'natural philosophy' by a certain Segner for having chosen this motif for its frontispiece, in order to fill the apprentice, whom he was ready to take into this temple, with 'a holy awe'.[6] Schiller in fact had already alluded to the inscription six years before writing the poem in his essay on 'The mission of Moses', where he applies it to the need of faith to remain esoteric.[7] But in the poem just quoted the application is surely much wider; nor need we indulge in much guesswork, for its message, which is meant to remain mysterious in the parable, is spelt out in another poem of the same year, 1795, and entitled 'Poesie des Lebens' ('The poetry of life'). It is ostensibly addressed to a friend, who, as I may put it, despises veils. He, we are told, is a stern realist who wants to see truth naked, *entblösst.* The effect of this uncompromising demand is as catastrophic as was the sacrilegious action of the youth in the temple:

Erschreckt von deinem ernsten Worte,
Entflieht der Liebesgötter Schar,
Der Musen Spiel verstummt, es ruhn der Horen Tänze,
Still trauernd nehmen ihre Kränze
Die Schwestergöttinnen vom schön gelockten Haar,

[6] *Critique of Judgement*, translated by James Creed Meredith (Oxford, 1952), p.179. The ultimate source of the inscription is Plutarch, *De Iside et Osiride,* 354C. Its background and ramifications in eighteenth-century thought and imagery are fully explored in Pierre Hadot, 'Zur Idee der Naturgeheimnisse', *Abhandlungen der Akademie der Wissenschaften und der Literatur in Mainz*, geistes- und sozialwissenschaftliche Klasse (1982), no.8, pp.3-33, where there is also an illustration of Segner's frontispiece commended by Kant. I should like to thank Professor Ernst Kitzinger for having drawn my attention to this article.

[7] *Die Sendung Moses, SW*, 4.792; Schiller also refers to the inscription in *Über das Erhabene (On the Sublime), SW*, 5.508.

Apoll zerbricht die goldne Leier,
Und Hermes seinen Wunderstab,
Des Traumes rosenfarbner Schleier
Fällt von des Lebens bleichem Antlitz ab.
Die Welt scheint, was sie ist, ein Grab.
Von seinen Augen nimmt die zauberische Binde
Cytherens Sohn; die Liebe sieht,
Sie sieht in ihrem Götterkinde
Den Sterblichen, erschrickt und flieht,
Der Schönheit Jugendbild veraltet,
Auf deinen Lippen selbst erkaltet
Der Liebe Kuss, und in der Freude Schwung
Ergreift dich die Versteinerung.

Alarmed by words of such severity
The flock of Cupids takes to flight at once.
The Muses cease to play, the Hours cease to dance,
The divine sisters take in silent grief
The charming garlands from their glorious locks.
Apollo breaks his golden lyre
And Hermes his miraculous staff.
The rosey-coloured veil of dream
Drops from the haggard face of life.
The world *seems* what it *is* –a grave.
From off his eyes Cythera's son will take
The enchanted bandage, love will *see*,
See in the heavenly offspring of the Gods
The mortal, shrinks away and flees,
The beauty that was youth grows old,
And on your very lips is chilled
The kiss of love, till in the sweep of joy
You will be turned to stone.

I believe there is no other poem by Schiller where the emotional meaning lies as close to the surface as in this didactic exhortation addressed to a materialist. We now know why the youth of Sais could never feel joy again after having lifted the veil from Truth. Knowledge of the truth is unbearable to us mortals. I fear Schiller has slightly veiled his stark message at the end of the parable by inserting the saving formula, 'woe to him who comes to Truth through guilt'. For it is always a guilty desire to seek more knowledge than is good for us.

I think I need not encroach too far on the psychoanalyst's prerogative if I add, on the basis of the other poem, that the knowledge Schiller means is what used to be called carnal knowledge.

> ... *die Liebe* sieht,
> *Sie sieht in ihrem Götterkinde*
> *Den Sterblichen, erschrickt und flieht.*

> ... love will *see*,
> See in the heavenly offspring of the Gods
> The mortal, shrinks away and flees.

Carnal knowledge, the act of love, leads to disillusionment and disenchantment. I think once we are alerted to the deeply rooted psychological conflict here expressed we find it again in various guises. Not unexpectedly, it surfaces in one of Schiller's most popular poems, 'Das Lied von der Glocke' ('The lay of the bell') of 1799, where it takes the form of homely wisdom but retains the image of the veil:

> *Drum prüfe, wer sich ewig bindet,*
> *Ob sich das Herz zum Herzen findet!*
> *Der Wahn ist kurz, die Reu ist lang.*
> *Lieblich in der Bräute Locken*
> *Spielt der jungfräuliche Kranz,*
> *Wenn die hellen Kirchenglocken*
> *Laden zu des Festes Glanz.*
> *Ach! des Lebens schönste Feier*
> *Endigt auch den Lebens-Mai,*
> *Mit dem Gürtel, mit dem Schleier*
> *Reisst der schöne Wahn entzwei.*

> Let him who binds himself forever
> Examine whether her heart matches his.
> The illusion is brief, the repentance long.
> Charming in the Virgin's locks
> Sits the lovely bridal wreath
> When the bright peal of the church bells
> Summons to the splendid celebration.
> Alas, the fairest feast of life

Also ends the May of life.
With the girdle and the veil
The fair illusion is also torn.

And finally, even more starkly, in a long poem entitled 'Kassandra' ('Cassandra') of 1802 where Schiller expresses his dread of reality in the most succinct stanzas:

Frommt's, den Schleier aufzuheben,
Wo das nahe Schrecknis droht?
Nur der Irrtum ist das Leben,
Und das Wissen ist der Tod.
Nimm, o nimm die traur'ge Klarheit,
Mir vom Aug den blut'gen Schein!
Schrecklich ist es, deiner Wahrheit
Sterbliches Gefäss zu sein.

Meine Blindheit gib mir wieder
Und den fröhlich dunkeln Sinn!
Nimmer sang ich freud'ge Lieder,
Seit ich deine *Stimme bin.*
Zukunft hast du mir gegeben,
Doch du nahmst den Augenblick,
Nahmst der Stunde fröhlich Leben;
Nimm dein falsch Geschenk zurück!

... Mir erscheint der Lenz vergebens,
Der die Erde festlich schmückt;
Wer erfreute sich des Lebens,
Der in seine Tiefen blickt!

Is it meet to lift the veil
Where the horror threatens nigh?
Error alone is life
And knowledge is death.
Take, O take the sad awareness
From my eyes, that sight of blood.
It is terrible to be the mortal vessel
Of your truth!

Let me have again my blindness
And the cheerful dreamy mind.
Never have I sung with joy
Since I have become *your* voice.
You have given me the future,
But you robbed me of the now
Of the gaity of the hour.
Take back your false present!

... Springtime that adorns the earth
Comes in vain to me;
Who would enjoy life
Who gazes into its depths?

Once more the deep pessimism of the lines is associated with the erotic, as Cassandra confesses:

... Gerne möcht ich mit dem Gatten
In die heimsche Wohnung ziehn;
Doch es tritt ein stygscher Schatten
Nächtlich zwischen mich und ihn.

... Gladly I would follow the spouse
To the dwelling of his home;
But a shadow from Styx
Steps every night between him and me.

'Kassandra' may be seen as a dramatic, not a confessional poem, but the same dread of reality breaks through in other creations, such as in the famous ballad of 'Der Taucher' ('The diver', 1797) who accepts the king's challenge and jumps into the whirlpool after a beaker to return exclaiming:

'Lang lebe der König! Es freue sich,
Wer da atmet im rosichten Licht.
Da unten aber ist's fürchterlich,
Und der Mensch versuche die Götter nicht,
Und begehre nimmer und nimmer zu schauen,
Was sie gnädig bedecken mit Nacht und Grauen.'

'Long live the King – and let those rejoice
Who breathe in rosy light.
But down there it is fearful,
And let man never challenge the gods,
And never, never, desire to see
What their mercy hides in night and gloom.'

There is no literal veil here, but the merciful veiling of the horrors of the deep which we should never want to behold.

Even when writing a dithyrambic drinking song ('Dithyrambe', 1796) the same thought could not be kept at bay. When the poet has joined the feast of the gods they call on Hebe to hand him the cup and to sprinkle his eyes with heavenly dew so that he cannot see the hated Styx and believes himself to be one of them.

Netz ihm die Augen mit himmlischem Taue,
Dass er den Styx, den verhassten, nicht schaue,
Einer der Unsern sich dünke zu sein.

Sprinkle his eyes with heavenly dew
So that he does not see hateful Styx
And believes himself to be one of us.

Remembering that it was this same man who wrote the ecstatic drinking song of the 'Ode to joy' (1785) immortalized by Beethoven, you may agree that there is here a psychological riddle which has not always been acknowledged by Schiller's admirers or indeed by his detractors. The latter have sometimes dismissed him as a high-minded but naive idealist whose preachings bordered on the platitudinous. But this facile view obviously does not quite square with the passages I have quoted so far. One rarely connects a naive idealism with an insistence on the sceptical wisdom that ignorance is bliss. The denial of reality, the attitude nowadays called 'escapism', turns out to be inseparable from his message, which often comes out more starkly in his poems than in his philosophical prose. This element of dread, almost of revulsion, from life in the raw may well spring from psychological tensions he learned to master and utilize in the course of his brief creative life, beset as it was by hardship and illness.

The poems I have introduced so far all date from the time of Schiller's maturity. Clearly we must turn to his earlier products if we want to trace their psychological roots. Now the tone and character of his early works differ notoriously from his later masterpieces. Made rebellious by the strict discipline of the military academy which he was compelled to attend by the tyrannical Duke of Württemberg, he startled the German public at the age of twenty-one by his revolutionary play *Die Räuber* (*The Robbers*, or rather *The Brigands*), soon to be followed by a series of some thirty lyrical poems of equal turbulence and daring.

There is much in these youthful products of 1781 which is slightly embarrassing, and some of the worst lines and stanzas were later eliminated by the poet himself before he incorporated these early effusions in his collected works. Yet we must take note of the opinion of a recent critic, Professor Herman Weigand of Yale University, that these poems of Schiller's youth, though crude and raw as poems, are, psychologically considered, the most interesting product of Schiller's career. Using the frank language of our age, Professor Weigand justifies his verdict by the observation that 'the male sex drive, now naked, now cerebrally masked, exhibits itself to full view in the most characteristic poems of the period'. It is easy to see what he has in mind when one reads the rather awful hymn on virile potency originally entitled 'Kastraten und Männer' ('Eunuchs and men'), but also the arch stanzas of 'The chariot of Venus', 'The triumph of love' and some of the Odes to Laura, with their undisguised celebration of sexual ecstasy; or if one remembers the crass and bawdy episodes in *Die Räuber* such as the raping of nuns. One might also agree with Professor Weigand when he says that 'desire stalks also through the later poems and essays by Schiller as the contaminating drive to be renounced in favour of disinterested contemplation'. I am less convinced, perhaps, by the same author's diagnosis that 'in the experience of sex the moral dichotomy of duty and impulse confronted Schiller in the core of his personality'.[8] Less convinced, because it seems to me that the poems of his later period I have quoted illustrate a conflict that goes deeper than the moral

[8] Herman J. Weigand, 'Schiller: Transfiguration of a Titan', in *A Schiller Symposium in Observance of the Bicentenary of Schiller's Birth*, ed. A. Leslie Wilson (Austin, Texas, 1960), p.93.

dichotomy between impulse and duty.

As we have seen, it is not so much ordinary normal desire which pervades his poetry but a desire counterbalanced by revulsion. To be sure, this flight from the flesh might be connected with orthodox Christian teaching about original sin and the Fall, and it is true that the story of the Fall also figures in one of the frantic love poems to Laura I have mentioned, a poem in which the symbol of the veil also makes its appearance.

It is entitled the 'Das Geheimnis der Reminiszenz' ('The secret of reminiscence') and draws on the Platonic conceit according to which male and female were once one single being. In that paradisaical state the veil is allowed to tear without revealing horrors.

Unsern Augen riss der Dinge Schleier,
Unsre Blicke, flammender und freier,
Sahen in der Schöpfung Labyrinthen ...

Before our eyes the veil of reality was torn,
And our gaze, more fiery and more free,
Peered into the labyrinth of creation ...

But that, remember, was before the Fall. For the poem ends with an ambiguous allusion to the forbidden fruit – ambiguous, because it almost reads like an apotheosis of Eve's sin:

Laura – majestätisch anzuschauen
Stand ein Baum in Edens Blumenauen;
'Seine Frucht vernein ich eurem Gaume,
Wisst! der Apfel an dem Wunderbaume
Labt – mit Göttertraume.'

Laura – weine unsres Glückes Wunde! –
Saftig war der Apfel ihrem Munde –
Bald – als sie sich unschuldsvoll umrollten –
Sieh! – wie Flammen ihr Gesicht vergoldten! –
Und die Teufel schmollten.

Laura, majestic to behold
There stood a tree in the flowering groves of Paradise.
'I deny its fruit to your palate,
Know, the apple of this miraculous tree
Gives you the bliss of a divine dream.'

Laura – weep at the wound of our happiness!
How juicy was the apple in their mouth –
But soon – when they tumbled innocently in the grass –
Look – how the flames gilded their faces –
And the devils grinned.[9]

The flames, I suppose, are those of hell, because the innocent tumble did not remain innocent. But the mood of that ending is far from Christian.

Schiller had indeed wanted to become a Protestant pastor, but since theology was not an option offered in the duke's academy he reluctantly chose a medical career. We can only speculate whether his experiences in the dissecting room and during his brief spell as a regimental surgeon contributed to his conviction that it is better not to look behind the veil. What we know is that the intellectual doctrine of a benevolent and admired physician had a lasting influence on his outlook.[10]

I make no apology for alluding to this system of ideas in a lecture devoted to a psychological interpretation, for if I need authority for this move I find it in the writings of my erstwhile mentor Ernst Kris, who stressed that we must never lose sight of the special historical conditions which determine the expression of psychological tensions.[11] In Schiller's case I have no doubt that his studies enabled him to formulate and objectify his dominant conflict.

Schiller's medical dissertation was entitled 'On the connection between man's animal nature and his spiritual nature'. It was a subject of the most urgent topicality in the Age of Reason, when La

[9] 'Und die Teufel schmollten' does not mean 'and the devils sulked' as it would in modern German, but that they smiled or grinned. See Heinrich Viehoff, *Schillers Gedichte erläutert* (Stuttgart, 1887), p.77.

[10] For this and the following see Kenneth Dewhurst and Nigel Reeves, *Friedrich Schiller: Medicine, Psychology and Literature* (Oxford, 1978), to which I am much indebted.

[11] *Psychoanalytic Explorations in Art* (New York, 1952), p.29.

Mettrie had proclaimed that man was a machine, and when Holbach and Helvetius had propagated their various materialistic systems. Responding to this challenge, Schiller's teachers preferred the doctrines of the Scottish philosophers Ferguson, Hutcheson and Reid, who went their own way in interpreting the relation between the life of the body, the life of the spirit and that of the universe. What matters to me in this welter of ideas is the place assigned to instinct in the household of nature. Instinct, or whatever alternative term is chosen,[12] dominates the existence of animals and also holds its sway over human actions and feelings however much it may come into conflict with pure spirituality. But in many of these systems instinct is more than a principle of life; by a bold imaginative leap it is identified with the promptings of nature in a pantheistic universe in which even the mutual attractions of the planets can be seen as a manifestation of sympathy.[13] Remember the 'Ode to joy' again: 'was den grossen Ring bewohnet, huldiget der Sympathie' ('whatever inhabits the great circle pays tribute to sympathy'). Now in this unified vision which contains echoes of Plato and the mystics, instinct, the sex drive if you prefer the word, is revealed as a cosmic principle, and this helps to account for the hyperbolic language of Schiller's early love poems, such as his 'Phantasie an Laura' ('Phantasy for Laur') of 1781:

Meine Laura! Nenne mir den Wirbel,
Der an Körper Körper mächtig reisst,
Nenne, meine Laura, mir den Zauber,
Der zum Geist gewaltig zwingt den Geist!

Sieh! er lehrt die schwebenden Planeten
Ewgen Ringgangs um die Sonne fliehn ...

My dear Laura, tell me of the vortex
Which with mighty pull our bodies joins.
Tell me my dear Laura of the magic
Which compels the spirit to the spirit.

[12] Cf. Wolfgang Düssing, *Begriffsregister zu den theoretischen Schriften*, issued as an appendix to *SW*.

[13] The transition seemed no doubt natural from the ancient cosmological doctrine that it is 'love that moves the heavens' to the identification of this mutual love with Newtonian attraction.

See, it teaches all the hovering planets
How to dance for ever round the sun ...

and so on. It is this cosmic force, as the poet assures his beloved, which animates them both in their love and which can only perish with the universe itself.

And yet this glorification of sexual love as a law of nature must have consequences which are bound to trouble a reflecting nature such as Schiller's. All the ecstatic celebration of instinct could not possibly conceal from him the logical consequence that, if it is instinct which drives the world around, we are no more than puppets, creatures of necessity or chance.

It was this negative consequence of the philosophy of man that was drawn by the French materialists and that must have troubled Schiller as it troubled so many others.[14] I believe that it is this threat to human freedom, more than the conflict between impulse and duty, that survives in the poems I quoted at the outset. Remember that as soon as love 'sees' it 'sees a mortal, shrinks away and flees'. The truth of our animal nature is that terrible truth that must be veiled. This feeling of revulsion, an almost Swiftian disgust, is most openly expressed in the soliloquies of the villain Franz Moor in *Die Räuber*, Franz Moor the libertine who justifies his nefarious plans of fratricide and patricide by asking what could possibly render life sacred: 'not, surely, the *actus* itself by which it originated, as if it were more than a bestial process to satisfy bestial desires ...'. 'Look,' he continues, 'that is the whole mystery which you veil with a fog of sanctity in order to take advantage of our fearfulness.'[15] Franz, as you notice, has seen nature in the raw behind the pious veil, and what he has seen is nothing but bestiality – a bestiality which seems to obsess him, for he returns to the topic later in the play, where he muses that the existence of most people may depend on the heat of a summer afternoon, the attractive look of bed linen or the horizontal position of a scullery belle which may have prompted the bestial desire that led to the birth of a human being.[16]

[14] In his early report on the psychological afflictions of a fellow student, Grammont, Schiller attributes the deep depressions of his patient largely to his tormenting metaphysical doubts. See *Schillers Leben dokumentarisch*, ed. Walter Hoyer (Cologne, 1967), p.47.

[15] 'Sehet also, das ist die ganze Hexerei, die ihr mit einem heiligen Nebel verschleiert, unsre Furchtsamkeit zu missbrauchen' (act 1, scene 1).

[16] Act 4, scene 2.

It may be objected that it is nothing less than monstrous to attribute to the playwright the opinions he put into the mouth of his grotesque villain, and of course that is true. But then Schiller himself had written in the revealing preface to the first edition of the play that it behoves any playwright to roam for a while through his own nocturnal labyrinths ('augenblicklich seine nächtlichen Labyrinthe durchwandern'), and it is down there he found his Franz Moor. Moreover, in a famous letter to Reinwald of 14 April 1783 which exhibits all the intuitive self-knowledge Freud concedes to the poet, Schiller writes, in discussing his play *Don Carlos*, that 'all creations of our imagination are nothing but our own self'.

It suits my trend of thought that Schiller explains in that same confessional letter that he regards love as no more than a happy deception. 'Is it really for another being that we tremble, glow and melt? Certainly not. We suffer all this only for ourselves, for the I of which the other creature is the mirror.'[17]

Whatever the immediate experience may have been which prompted this outburst – and we hear from contemporaries that the original Laura was not a very prepossessing person[18] – it is not with Schiller's various emotional entanglements that I can be here concerned, but with his reactions to the vicissitudes of a hard and unsettled life. There is no more telling document of this intellectual and emotional ferment than the *Philosophical Letters* of 1786. They are cast in the form of a correspondence between two friends, Julius and Raphael, who represent the two poles of Schiller's mental universe. The first is an enthusiastic youth, the second a maturer person who has deprived the young man of his religious ideals. In the first of the letters, therefore, Julius reproaches Raphael: 'you have stolen the faith that gave me peace ... a thousand things were venerable to me, ere your sorry wisdom stripped them naked'. In the second letter, the complaint mounts to a crescendo. 'Our philosophy is the fateful curiosity of Oedipus who never ceased asking till the terrible oracle was solved: "may you never learn who you are".'[19] It is a remark which may well make a psychoanalyst prick up his ears, and that not

[17] *Schillers Leben dokumentarisch*, pp.111-12.

[18] Her name was Luise Dorothea Vischer; cf. the index to *Schillers Leben dokumentarisch*. For Schiller's relation to women see also Emil Staiger, *Friedrich Schiller* (Zürich, 1967), pp.17-18.

[19] *SW*, 5.339, 341.

only because of the mythological allusion. To ask who we are – one might say – is to ask how we were made, and the answer must be that of Franz Moor, the terrible secret that must remain hidden behind the veil.

True, in the correspondence a few soothing words from his friend encourage the young enthusiast to substitute for this sorry wisdom a grandiose account of a pantheistic theosophy which certainly provided the *raison d'être* for the correspondence. But this poetic effusion is yet placed between quotation marks, as it were. The correspondence ends with a friendly but cool response from the older friend who preaches intellectual humility.

In thus distancing his own vision of a consoling metaphysics Schiller continued on the path we saw him pursuing in his interpretation of love. I previously referred to the denial of reality. Now we must call it by its other name, the acceptance of fantasy. Whatever may lie behind the veil, we must cherish man's capacity to live in such a dream-world.

Perhaps the first of the poems in which this message is spelt out explicitly is the one appropriately called 'Resignation' (1781), and, equally appropriately, it settles account with the Christian hope. Here the poet imagines himself confronting the ultimate Judge and claiming his reward for having sacrificed all the pleasure of life to the hope of a happy afterlife, defying and despising, as he did, the mockery of his sceptical fellow-creatures. But the verdict of an invisible genius decrees otherwise.

'Zwei Blumen,' rief er, 'hört es, Menschenkinder,
Zwei Blumen blühen für den weisen Finder,
Sie heissen Hoffnung *und* Genuss.
Wer dieser Blumen Eine brach, begehre
Die andre Schwester nicht.
Geniesse, wer nicht glauben kann. Die Lehre
Ist ewig wie die Welt. Wer glauben kann, entbehre!'

'Two flowers,' quoth he, 'listen human children,
Two flowers blossom for the wise who find them.
Hope is the name of one, the other's *Pleasure*.
He who picks one of them must not demand
To pick the other;
Let him who is short of faith have pleasure –

that lesson is old as history.
He who has faith must practice renunciation.'

Renunciation of pleasure, indeed abstention is now his message in 'Einer jungen Freundin ins Stammbuch' ('Lines written into the album of a young lady', 1788), no less poignant in hindsight for being addressed to his future wife Charlotte von Lengenfeld:

Sei glücklich in dem lieblichen Betruge,
Nie stürze von des Traumes stolzem Fluge
Ein trauriges Erwachen dich herab.
Den Blumen gleich, die deine Beete schmücken,
So pflanze sie – nur den entfernten Blicken;
Betrachte *sie – doch* pflücke *sie nicht* ab!
Geschaffen, nur die Augen zu vergnügen,
Welk werden sie zu deinen Füssen liegen,
Je näher dir – je näher ihrem Grab!

Be happy in the charm of this deception,
And may a sad awakening never hurl you
Down from the soaring boldness of this dream.
Just like the flowers which adorn your garden
Which you have planted for the distant gaze,
Enjoy their looks but do not ever break them.
Created to give pleasure to the eyes
They will lie dead and faded at your feet.
The nearer you, the nearer to their grave.

Two years later, in his long and fine poem 'Die Götter Griechenlands' ('The Gods of Greece', 1788), Schiller still deplores our loss of innocence, our loss of the poetic illusion he finds enshrined in pagan mythology before science shattered its fabric:

Da der Dichtkunst malerische Hülle
Sich noch lieblich um die Wahrheit wand,
Durch die Schöpfung floss da Lebensfülle,
Und was nie empfinden wird, empfand.

When the painted cloth of poetry
Was charmingly still wrapped around the truth,
Then creation still pulsated with life
And what never will feel, still felt.

How can we recover that feeling in a Newtonian Universe?

Unbewusst der Freuden, die sie schenket,
Nie entzückt von ihrer Trefflichkeit,
Nie gewahr des Armes, der sie lenket,
Reicher nie durch meine Dankbarkeit,
Fühllos selbst für ihres Künstlers Ehre,
Gleich dem todten Schlag der Pendeluhr,
Dient sie knechtisch dem Gesetz der Schwere,
Die entgötterte Natur.

Not aware of all the joys it gives us,
Not delighted by its own perfection,
Never knowing of the arm that guides it,
Not enriched by my own gratitude,
Senseless to the honour of its Maker,
Like the regular striking of the clock
Slave to the iron laws of gravity,
Nature is bereft of all the Gods.

Once more, increasing knowledge had spelt unhappiness for man; for now he confronts an alien Universe. Once, he had felt kinship with the pagan gods; now the transcendent divinity is out of his reach.

Bürger des Olymps konnt ich erreichen,
Jenem Gotte, den sein Marmor preist,
Konnte einst der hohe Bildner gleichen:
Was ist neben Dir der höchste Geist
Derer welche Sterbliche gebaren?
Nur der Würmer Erster, Edelster,
Da die Götter menschlicher noch waren,
Waren Menschen göttlicher.

To Olympus I might still aspire,
And the God his marble celebrates
Could the noble sculptor try to equal.
What is compared to you the highest spirit
Of the spirits born of mortal men?
Of the worms perhaps the first, most noble.
When the Gods had more humanity
Humans were more godly too.

Winston Churchill once said that if indeed we are all worms, he wanted to be a glow-worm. Schiller certainly shared his aspiration. And he nourished the hope that the required glow could be derived from the arts. In a long rhapsodic poem of 1789, 'Die Künstler' ('The artists'), he sketched a vast canvas of the rise of mankind from animal status through the guidance of the arts.

The arts it was which paved the way towards the sublimation of instinct and turned a mere drive into love.

Dass von des Sinnes niederm Triebe
Der Liebe bessrer Keim sich schied,
Dankt er dem ersten Hirtenlied.
Geadelt zur Gedankenwürde,
Floss die verschämtere Begierde
Melodisch aus des Sängers Mund.

Thanks to the first of shepherd's songs
The better germ of love divided
From sensuality's low drive.
For now, more bashfully, desire,
Raised to the noble dignity of thought,
Melodiously flowed from the singer's lips.

Or, to revert to my leitmotif:

Ihr führet uns im Brautgewande
Die fürchterliche Unbekannte,
Die unerweichte Parze vor.

You show us the dreaded Unknown
The pitiless Fate
Dressed as a bride.

I need not remind you that the bridal garb is the veil.

But in this poem, which we may describe as the last of Schiller's youth, written, as it was, in his thirtieth year, the hope is still expressed that the artist will not only veil our animal nature, he will ultimately lead mankind beyond this status. The experience of Beauty in Art will make him ripe, in distant millennia, also to contemplate Truth without a veil; or to put it in Schiller's favourite idiom of mythological metaphor, once man is of age, Venus will cast off her veil and stand before him as Urania, with a fiery crown.[20]

But these enthusiastic intimations of an aesthetic millennium date from the year before Schiller seriously began the study of Kant, whose ideas were henceforth to dominate his reflections. One of the results of Kant's *Critiques* must have been of immediate relevance to Schiller's psychological conflicts. He was assured that neither the claims of materialism nor those of religion could be tested in the Court of Reason. Their alleged proofs were bound to be spurious. We cannot ever know 'the thing in itself'.

One of the first poems Schiller wrote when he resumed poetry after an interval of some six years was a farewell to his youth and its ideals, 'Die Ideale' (1795).

Die Wirklichkeit mit ihren Schranken
Umlagert den gebundnen Geist,
Sie stürzt, die Schöpfung der Gedanken,
Der Dichtung schöner Flor zerreisst.

Reality with all its barriers
Besets the spirit in its chains.
What thought created now collapses
And Poetry's fair veil is torn.

What saves the poet from despair in this progressive disillusionment, when after a short springtime even the dream of love escapes, are two consoling companions – friendship, and work.

Beschäftigung, die nie ermattet,
Die langsam schafft, doch nie zerstört,
Die zu dem Bau der Ewigkeiten
Zwar Sandkorn nur für Sandkorn reicht,
Doch von der grossen Schuld der Zeiten
Minuten, Tage, Jahre streicht.

Activity, that never flags,
That creates but slowly but never destroys.

[20] *Sie selbst, die sanfte Cypria,*
Umleuchtet von der Feuerkrone,
Steht dann vor ihrem mündgen Sohne,
Entschleiert – als Urania …

True, to the building of Eternity
It merely adds its grain of sand
And yet – of the great debt of ages
It cancels minutes, days, and years.

I cannot think of a more fitting description of that watershed that separates maturity from youth. No doubt his maturity also owes something to Kant's influence, to the *Critique of Practical Reason* with its emphasis on duty. He had also learned from Kant not to dismiss belief in values as mere illusion. True, it could not be justified by scientific proof, but it could be justified by faith as a postulate.

As Schiller was to write in the beautiful poem 'Die Sehnsucht' ('Longing', 1801).

Du musst glauben, du musst wagen,
Denn die Götter leihn kein Pfand;
Nur ein Wunder kann dich tragen
In das schöne Wunderland.

You must have faith, you must be bold,
Because the Gods don't give a pledge;
Only a miracle can take you
To the fair land of miracles.

For Schiller, of course, the land of miracles is still the realm of poetry, of art, which is also the realm of freedom because here man is liberated from the chains of necessity and the servitude to desire. He had enthusiastically accepted Kant's conception of the beautiful as disinterested pleasure, a pleasure totally divorced from selfish desire or interest. That vision of man's ability to cut the chains that kept the body in bondage allowed him to celebrate what I have called the denial of reality, first manifested in the play instinct as the most precious gift life can offer, the gift of freedom.

I cannot follow here the road which leads from this point directly to the core of Schiller's philosophy of art;[21] the thesis which conceives of art as what one might call the illusion of the illusionless,

[21] The best and most sympathetic introduction to Schiller's aesthetics known to me is the bilingual and richly annotated edition of the letters *On the Aesthetic Education of Man* by Elizabeth M. Wilkinson and L.A. Willoughby (Oxford, 1967), with its masterly introduction.

the knowing enjoyment of fiction and of the willing suspension of disbelief. What I rather want to stress in my context is the link which Schiller's aesthetic creed still maintains with what I have called his psychological conflicts. I see this link in his puritanical insistence on abstention, his rigorous separation of the aesthetic emotion from any kind of sensuous indulgence.

That he dismissed with scorn Edmund Burke's derivation of our sense of beauty from the erotic instinct of self-propagation cannot surprise us.[22] But his description of a concert hall during the playing of ravishing music is again revealing for the disgust it conveys.

> However much noise there may be in a concert hall, everybody will be 'all ears' as soon as a sweetly melting passage is performed. An expression of sensuality bordering on the brutish usually appears on people's faces, the drunken eyes are watery, the open mouth is all desire, a lustful tremor seizes the whole body, the breath is rapid and faint, in short all the symptoms of inebriation appear – a clear proof that the senses are revelling but that the spirit, or the principle of freedom in man, has fallen prey to the sensuous impression.[23]

This almost Manichean dualism pervades the most accomplished of Schiller's philosophical poems, which he originally called 'Das Reich der Schatten' ('The realm of shadows'), but published later as 'Das Ideal und das Leben' ('Ideal and life', 1795).[24] It is a celebration of both renunciation and illusion:

Wollt ihr schon auf Erden Göttern gleichen,
Frei sein in des Todes Reichen,
Brechet nicht von seines Gartens Frucht!
An dem Scheine mag der Blick sich weiden,
Des Genusses wandelbare Freuden
Rächet schleunig der Begierde Flucht.
Selbst der Styx, der neunfach sie umwindet,
Wehrt die Rückkehr Ceres Tochter nicht;
Nach dem Apfel greift sie, und es bindet
Ewig sie des Orkus Pflicht.

[22] In his letter to Goethe of 12 September 1794 Schiller attributes this Burkean view to his visitor Ramdohr.

[23] *Über das Pathetische (On the Pathetic)*, *SW*, 5.516.

[24] I ventured to attempt a verse translation of two of its stanzas in my lecture on Raphael's Madonna della Sedia, *Norm and Form* (Oxford, 1966), p.70.

If on earth you strive to equal God,
To be free in the domains of death,
Never in its garden pick the fruit.
While the gaze may revel in their sight
Rapidly the changing joys of pleasure
Are revenged, as the desire flees.
Even Styx, which winds its ninefold loops,
Could Demeter's daughter not imprison;
When she grasped the apple, then for ever
To the laws of Orcus she was slave.

This insistence on the instability of earthly pleasures, which only lead to the loss of desire, serves to show that there is more than one thread that links Schiller's mature Kantian philosophy with the ideas of his formative years. Indeed Kenneth Dewhurst and Nigel Reeves, in their edition and translation of Schiller's early medical writings,[25] have convinced me that many of his early conceptions survived the conversion to Kant. We would expect such a continuity when looking at Schiller's development in a psychological light. We have learned from psychoanalysis to pay attention to this element of continuity in change which so often marks the creations of great minds.

In his first treatise on the links between man's animal nature and his spiritual nature Schiller had enlarged on the fitfulness of the animal impulses, which go through a cycle of tension and release. He speaks of *Nachlass*, relaxation, that follows the satisfaction of instincts, which serves the purposes of nature no less certainly than does the preceding climax of tension.

That warning of revulsion, that dread of what lies behind the veil, therefore, which animates the poems of Schiller's Kantian period, and which I quoted at the beginning, is still connected with his theoretical and emotional view of the condition of man. In his perceptive book on Schiller, Emil Staiger has emphasized how harshly Schiller views the realities of existence in that very poem on 'Ideal and life'.[26]

If the harshness sometimes appears to be mitigated in Schiller's later works, the change must be attributed to the second of the major

[25] Cited note 10 above.
[26] Cited note 18 above.

influences he experienced during the years that still remained to him. I am of course speaking of Goethe. The story of this friendship, and its reflections in their correspondence and in their joint epigrams, belongs to the most moving episodes of literary history. We have Goethe's own words for it that it was he who weaned Schiller of his dread of implacable Nature. At least that is what he wrote in 1817, twelve years after Schiller's death, when he looked back on the beginnings of their friendship in 1794 after a prolonged period of mutual distrust. 'Schiller,' wrote Goethe, 'preached the gospel of Freedom. I did not want the rights of Nature to be curtailed. Maybe it was his friendly feeling towards me rather than genuine conviction that made him not speak of the Good Mother in his Aesthetic Letters with the same harsh expressions which had rendered his essay on Grace and Dignity so hateful to me.'[27]

'Hateful', 'verhasst', is a strong word to use, but there are indeed passages in that long and difficult treatise *Über Anmut und Würde (On Grace and Dignity)* in which sensuality is bluntly equated with bestiality and painted in the same lurid colours we encountered in Schiller's description of the effects of music.[28] Even more rigorous, if that is possible, is Schiller's rejection of any compromise with the demands of Nature in the companion treatise *Über das Erhabene (On the Sublime)*, where even the veil is condemned as a concession to human weakness:

> Away, then, with the misconceived delicacy and the soft effeminating taste that throws a veil over the stern countenance of reality, and that, in order to curry favour with the senses, utters lies about a pretended harmony between well-being and moral behaviour, of which the real world shows no trace. Let us confront evil fate face to face ... [29]

Here speaks the dramatist, who needs the uncompromising

[27] *Einwirkungen der neuern Philosophie*, in *Zur Naturwissenschaft im Allgemeinen, Goethes Werke*, ed. Dorothea Kuhn and Rike Wankmüller (Munich, 1953-), 13.28-9. There is a parallel account in Goethe's *Annalen oder Tag- und Jahreshefte* on the year 1794, in which Goethe confesses to have suspected certain 'harsh passages' in *Über Anmut und Würde (On Grace and Dignity)* to have been aimed at him, but to have felt that matters were even worse if that was not the case, for then the enormous gulf that separated his mode of thinking from that of Schiller was even more apparent.

[28] *SW*, 5.462-3.

[29] *SW*, 5.806.

acceptance of harsh reality, rather than the lyrical poet. But even in the final of Schiller's *Letters on the Aesthetic Education of Man*, his principal philosophical work, the concession which Goethe remembered concerns, at the most the form, not the content, of Schiller's words. 'Taste,' he writes, 'spreads its softening veil over our physical needs which, in their naked form, offend against the dignity of free spirits and thus hides from us our degrading kinship with matter behind a charming phantom of freedom.'[30]

Remember what Franz Moor had said in his cynical musings on the sexual act when he sneered at those who veil bestial reality with a fog of sanctity. Not that Schiller here sides with his villain, if he ever did; he is grateful for the existence of the veil; he wants reality to be hidden from us, not, as Franz Moor alleges, because of religious fears, but because of his persistent dread which, as we have seen, he continued to express in the poems of the same year that saw the completion of the Aesthetic Letters.

Yet there is also a poem, 'Die Weltweisen' ('The Philosophers', 1795), from the year in which he published 'The image of Sais' and 'The poetry of life', the first full year of his friendship with Goethe, in which we may see a concession to Goethe's plea for Nature, the Good Mother. It is a humorous poem in which Schiller puts the philosophers in their place because their speculations will never change art or reality:

Doch weil, was ein Professor spricht,
Nicht gleich zu Allen dringet,
So übt Natur die Mutterpflicht
Und sorgt, dass nie die Kette bricht,
Und dass der Reif nie springet.
Einstweilen, bis den Bau der Welt
Philosophie zusammenhält,
Erhält sie das Getriebe
Durch Hunger und durch Liebe.

[30] 'Dafür breitet er über das physische Bedürfnis, das in seiner nackten Gestalt die Würde freier Geister beleidigt, seinen mildernden Schleier aus und verbirgt uns die entehrende Verwandtschaft mit dem Stoff in einem lieblichen Blendwerk von Freiheit.' I have somewhat departed from the translation by Wilkinson and Willoughby (p.218), who ingeniously render 'mildernder Schleier' as 'veil of decorum' and 'Blendwerk' as 'illusion'. But the latter German term carries stronger overtones; it is most often associated with black magic (*Blendwerk der Hölle*), and so I have proposed 'phantom'.

But since what a professor says
Will not be heard by all,
Nature a mother's duty does,
Makes certain that the chains don't break
And that the ring won't burst.
Pro tem before philosophers
Can make the world cohere,
She keeps the works in motion
Through hunger and through love.

You will not be surprised to learn that Sigmund Freud specially liked to quote these lines. Not that the sentiment expressed contradicts Schiller's other utterances; he had always acknowledged the power of Nature over her own dominion, which he saw as the domain of Necessity, of the law rather than of freedom. But maybe the contact with Goethe had really made him see that not everybody was as deeply disturbed by the pressures of instinct as he was. In the poem 'The realm of shadows', from which I have quoted, he had still posed the dilemma of human existence in the most uncompromising terms. Man, he said, had only the agonizing choice between sensual pleasure and spiritual peace; only Jove could combine them both.[31] The Father of the Gods was obviously not troubled in his conscience while he enjoyed the embraces of his various loves in the most unlikely disguises. In Goethe, Schiller encountered, if not Jove himself, at least a human being whose serenity did not seem to be broken by his sensuality. The author of the joyfully erotic *Roman Elegies* showed no signs of being troubled by the degrading kinship with matter.

This contact with an undivided soul had a healing effect on Schiller.[32] He began to reflect on the difference he had found between their various gifts and modes of creation and used the result of this introspection for a typology of poets, *Über naïve und sentimentalische Dichtung (On Naive and Sentimental Poetry)*, in which

[31] *Zwischen Sinnenglück und Seelenfrieden*
Bleibt dem Menschen nur die bange Wahl;
Auf der Stirn des hohen Uraniden
Leuchtet ihr vermählter Strahl.

[32] In her Special Taylorian Lecture *Schiller, Poet or Philosopher?* (Oxford, 1961), Elizabeth M. Wilkinson speaks of the 'healing give and take' of this friendship.

Goethe, as the naive and unbroken genius, was to be ranked with the Greeks and indeed with Nature herself, while Schiller could still assign a place to himself as what he calls a *sentimentalischer*, a reflecting author, one, we surmise, who had peered behind the veil and shrunk back. I have called Schiller's poem 'Kassandra', which I quoted for its most uncompromising pessimism, a dramatic poem, the poem which links the lifting of the veil with the assertion that error only is life and knowledge death. It is perhaps dramatic in the sense of being a monologue, expressed in the full awareness that, like the Greek seer, he experienced what other people were spared.

It so happens that Goethe himself also used the image of the veil, in a highly significant context, a poem of dedication which was to introduce his mystical stanzas 'Die Geheimnisse' ('The secrets'), and which he later used as the dedication of his collected poems. Following the ancient precedent of describing allegorical encounters,[33] it tells of the poet's cheerful ascent on a spring morning when he is met by a divine figure who appears out of the gathering mists. He addresses her as the object of all his desire, the personification of Truth, and with a benevolent smile she stretches out her hands to gather in the fog that had covered the scene; she transforms it into a veil she now pulls from the landscape, handing it to the poet as her gift, with the promise that the happy man who receives it with a serene mind will never lack anything, for now he can work magic with that veil:

Aus Morgenduft gewebt und Sonnenklarheit
Der Dichtung Schleier aus der Hand der Wahrheit.

Woven from morning haze and solar radiance,
The veil of poetry from the hand of truth.

Truth bestows the magic veil of poetry on happy and serene souls, not to cover the terrors of existence, merely to offer relief when the heat of the day becomes oppressive.[34]

[33] I have discussed such a correspondence in my article 'Goethe's "Zueignung" und Benivieni's "Amore" ', *Journal of the Warburg and Courtauld Institutes*, 1 (1937-8), though I probably over-emphasized the parallel.

[34] For Goethe's various uses of the symbol of the veil see Wilhelm Emrich, *Die Symbolik von Faust II* (Frankfurt am Main, 1964).

Goethe, who implicitly alluded to the motif of this Dedication in the untranslatable subtitle he gave to his autobiography – *Wahrheit und Dichtung*, which means both *Truth and Poetry* and *Truth and Fiction* – also transformed and transfigured the image of Schiller in the wonderful poetic monument he erected to his great friend, the 'Epilog zu Schillers Glocke' ('Epilogue to the lay of the bell'). He there pays tribute to Schiller's courage and faith which strove incessantly for 'the good to work, to grow and to prosper,/So that the day would dawn at last for the noble soul':

Damit das Gute wirke, wachse, fromme,
Damit der Tag dem Edlen endlich komme.

All of us who had a German education were conditioned by these lines to see in Schiller the optimistic idealist who had his eyes firmly fixed on the progress of humanity. It is with a shock that one comes to realize that this interpretation is flatly contradicted by Schiller's own profession of faith which he embodied in two poems, 'Die Worte des Glaubens' ('The words of faith', 1797) and 'Die Worte des Wahns' ('The words of delusion', 1799). While the first formulates his Kantian belief in the triad of Freedom, Virtue and Divinity, the other warns against the delusions of the age, the belief in the progress of mankind, in the justice of life and the possibility of ever discovering truth. Let this be the only one of Schiller's poems to be quoted in full.

Drei Worte hört man, bedeutungschwer,
Im Munde der Guten und Besten;
Sie schallen vergeblich, ihr Klang ist leer,
Sie können nicht helfen und trösten:
Verscherzt ist dem Menschen des Lebens Frucht,
Solang er die Schatten zu haschen sucht.

Solang er glaubt an die Goldene Zeit,
Wo das Rechte, das Gute wird siegen –
Das Rechte, das Gute führt ewig Streit,
Nie wird der Feind ihm erliegen,
Und erstickst du ihn nicht in den Lüften frei,
Stets wächst ihm die Kraft auf der Erde neu.

Solang er glaubt, dass das buhlende Glück
Sich dem Edeln vereinigen werde,
Dem Schlechten folgt est mit Liebesblick;
Nicht dem Guten gehöret die Erde:
Er ist ein Fremdling, er wandert aus
Und suchet ein unvergänglich Haus.

Solang er glaubt, dass dem ird'schen Verstand
Die Wahrheit je wird erscheinen;
Ihren Schleier hebt keine sterbliche Hand,
Wir können nur raten und meinen:
Du kerkerst den Geist in ein tönend Wort,
Doch der freie wandelt im Sturme fort.

Drum, edle Seele, entreiss dich dem Wahn,
Und den himmlischen Glauben bewahre!
Was kein Ohr vernahm, was die Augen nicht sahn,
Est ist dennoch das Schöne, das Wahre!
Es ist nicht draussen, da sucht es der Tor,
Es ist in *dir, du bringst es ewig hervor.*

Three words with a weighty meaning are heard
From the lips of the good and the best.
Their sound is hollow, they are spoken in vain,
They can neither help nor console,
And man must lose the fruits of his life
As long as these shadows he seeks to grasp.

While he places his trust in a golden age
When the right and the good will prevail.
The right, the good, are for ever at war,
Their opponent will never succumb.
For if you don't crush him right in mid-air
He will always gain strength as he touches the earth.

As long as he thinks that Fortuna, the whore,
Will ever side with the noble,
The villain she follows with loving eyes,
This earth is not owned by the good.
He is an alien, he leaves his home
And seeks an imperishable abode.

As long as he thinks that at any time
  The Truth will lie open to reason,
No mortal hand will lift that veil
  We can but guess and believe.
You imprison the spirit in high sounding words,
But it freely moves on like the storm that bloweth.

Hence, noble soul, these delusions discard
  But maintain the heavenly faith:
What no ear has heard, what no eyes have seen,
  It is yet the fair and the true.
It is not outside, where fools look for it,
It is within you, you are its eternal creator.

Once more Truth is represented as veiled, but here Schiller reverts to the original meaning of that legendary inscription under the image of Isis, 'I am all that is, and that was, and that shall be, and no mortal hath raised the veil from before my face'. It must have been, for him, a consoling insight.

* * *

The story goes that Greek playwrights who had dramatized a myth, say, of the Fall of Troy or of Oedipus, for the Athenian Dionysiaca, were sometimes greeted with calls of protest that this had nothing to do with Dionysus. I fear I have exposed myself to the criticism that what I present here has nothing to do with psychoanalysis. I certainly do not lay bare for you the origins of Schiller's conflicts behind the veil of his poetry and thought. I am not even convinced that such an enterprise would be possible or fruitful, given the distance of time and the scarcity of evidence. But maybe I might plead in conclusion that the very problems and conflicts which Schiller attempted to objectify were germane to Freud's thoughts and interests. The force of instinct, the function of illusion, the values of civilization in our efforts to come to terms with life, were constant themes in his metapsychological reflections. After all, as I said earlier, Freud himself stemmed from the tradition that had also formed Schiller. True, Freud never lacked the courage to lift the veil, but he also had the humility to confess in a letter to Yvette Guilbert about the secrets of her artistic achievements: 'we know so little' ('man weiss ja so wenig').[35]

[35] 8 March 1931, *Briefe, 1873-1939*, p.400.

CHAPTER FIVE

Psychoanalysis and Surrealism

S. Dresden

In 1900 – according to its title page: more accurately, in November 1899 – there appeared *The Interpretation of Dreams* by Dr Sigmund Freud of Vienna. At the time, its reception was one of mistrust and hilarity rather than of rapture: it was simply one more work by a middle-aged Viennese psychiatrist who enjoyed a measure of success in a small private practice but whose academic career proceeded only haltingly. Freud perhaps had arresting – certainly strange and disconcerting – ideas; and the circle that was to become the Vienna Psychoanalytical Society was admittedly founded not very long after the book's publication. The very fact, however, that the meetings of this circle were for years held at the founder's home, and under his strict personal guidance, revealed how small the first group of enthusiastic adherents must have been – adherents who were, in their own eyes, no more than pupils or disciples.

It was only after World War I that, like a tidal wave, the great fame of psychoanalysis began to engulf the arts and sciences everywhere. Only in France was its reception somewhat mixed (in spite of Marie Bonaparte). But *The Interpretation of Dreams*, which was initially paid such scant attention, had meanwhile come to be considered a revolutionary, if not seminal, work; indeed, it was felt that the year of its publication was no coincidence, and that, with the opening of the new century, entirely new avenues of thought were being opened up – thanks to Freud's analysis of the manifest and latent content of the unconscious, his recognition of wish-fulfilment in dreams, and all the rest of it. In other words, by the 1920s, it was being realized that great, possibly definitive progress had been made, in a field of enquiry whose fruitfulness seemed inexhaustible.

However, as soon as Freud's notions began to be employed in an amazing diversity of fields, as soon as Freud himself showed that he was constantly developing his ideas, offering them for discussion, and not entertaining a moment's hesitation in radically altering them, it was hardly possible to speak of psychoanalysis as such any longer. Side by side with Jung and Adler a host of sometimes extremely gifted researchers made their first appearance. Within the movement itself, which Freud would so dearly have liked to see firmly organized, schisms occurred again and again, and these – witness Lacan and the bitter conflicts in Parisian psychoanalytical groups – have continued right up to the present.

The initial picture offered by the Surrealist school is remarkably similar. On the eve of World War I, i.e. roughly a decade before it was possible to speak of a movement at all, one Marcel Duchamp – who is now appropriately being rediscovered – submitted a number of unusual objects for an exhibition in New York. They included a bicycle wheel, a glass tumbler bought in a department store, and an empty packet of cigarettes – all graced with his signature.

It can scarcely be denied that in these provocative exhibits – which had evidently been intended to elevate the most banal to the level of art – the first expression of the spirit of Dada was to be observed. During World War I, in Zurich and New York, and immediately afterwards in Paris and Berlin, the early Dadaists gathered for events which already assumed the nature of 'happenings', and gave utterance to their deep-seated contempt for anything that passed as culture. After the appalling violence and squalor of warfare this culture appeared to them hollow and devoid of sense. Protest, chance, and nonsense prevailed, and with this anti-art negativism was the order of the day.

But among the Paris Dadaists there were also several who in due course dissented. We need not dwell on the squabbles, the rows, the physical assaults even, which occurred in their ranks – although inevitably it was these that hit the headlines. What resulted was simply deep incomprehension on the part of the general public. In fact, like those equally weird early psychoanalytical publications, Surrealist doings were regarded with mockery and distaste. Here, too, it was a comparatively small circle of artists who came together both to preserve the negative nature of Dadaism and to elevate it into a positive doctrine. Of course, for 'elevate' one might prefer to substitute the German *aufheben*, and thereby recall Hegel. For it was not to be long before the Surrealists would mention his name repeatedly, and would – up to a point – rally under the banner of his philosophy.

We have, however, not as yet reached that stage in the story, even if it had been clear from the start that Surrealism did not wish to be merely a literary movement, or one comprising all the arts, or indeed to be exclusively inspired by any one philosophical, psychological, or political doctrine alone. What the Surrealists were actually after was the propagation of an all-embracing view of life and of the world, and the expression of this view in their works – whatever their nature. To this end they organized themselves into some curious forms of collectivism by 'communal writing' and (where possible) by anonymous publishing. In this way they not only attracted regular followers in various countries but they also literally constituted a school – perhaps even the only genuine school that French literature has ever known.

The minutes of the meetings of this school have been preserved (as have those of the Vienna Psychoanalytical Society). It is from them that the figure of André Breton emerges as an indubitable – though subsequently disputed – leader. Much like Freud, this leader would resort to excommunication (occasionally followed by reconciliation), and would dictate policies with an unflinching sense of his own superiority. It was hardly by chance, therefore, that on more than one occasion the big Surrealist manifestos were originally signed by large numbers of adherents but later reprinted under Breton's name alone. In these manifestos we may thus find political statements which had at first been widely accepted, but which some later on rejected, and which thus became the cause of further schisms. Nevertheless it is to those minutes that we must turn to discover how exactly Surrealism intended to achieve its ideals.

One particular statement in the second manifesto (1930) is especially revealing – or rather, shows most clearly the reasoning behind much that had at first appeared obscure. For it declared that there was 'a certain point in the human mind' at which life and death, the real and the imaginary, past and present, the communicable and the incommunicable, the lofty and the base, all ceased to be experienced as each other's opposites. 'We have to do away with those artificial antinomies,' it said. 'They have only hypocritically served to prevent unaccustomed emotion ...'.[1]

In this way the destructive negativism of Dada was being 'saved', as it were, by introducing a higher aim. But then in the course of the 1920s a number of things had happened in French Surrealism. For, political controversy apart, what was characteristic of the period was an intense attraction towards somnambulism and occultism, a plethora of newly-founded periodicals, a constant interest in the possibilities of new art-forms (such as film), and above all a complete liberation of thought and feeling. Accordingly, the keenest attention was focused on whatever seemed in essence to be remote from reason and reasonableness: the deeper, unconscious recesses of the mind, dreams, the mysterious and the miraculous; everything, in brief, that seemed strange and unfathomable. There was no more fear of those depths which medicine and psychiatry on one hand, and orthodox religion on the other, had always tried to camouflage – or at least to relegate to some remote corner of the human condition.

Even so superficial a description as this will have suggested certain parallel interests among psychoanalysts and Surrealists in the stratification of the human mind, and especially – to put it paradoxically – in the baseless fabric of the unconscious as a base for operation. It is a suggestion which may find its justification in the fact that, for a motto to his *Interpretation of Dreams*, Freud had chosen a line from the Aeneid which reads: 'Flectere si nequeo superos, Acheronta movebo' ('If I cannot move the gods above, I shall move the underworld'). Yet this inconspicuous detail also illustrates a profound contrast in attitude. No Surrealist would ever have dreamed of adorning any literary or even scholarly work of his with a Latin quotation.

But then parallels and contrasts are characteristic of many facets of the relationship between Freud and the Surrealists. There can be no doubt that the ideas of the Viennese psychiatrist were at first greatly admired in Surrealist circles, whereas subsequently disappointment and even aversion were registered. The famous visit to Freud of André Breton is a case in point. In 1921, while on holiday in the Tyrol, Breton decided to avail himself of the opportunity to pay

[1] André Breton, *Les manifestes du Surréalisme* (Paris, 1962), pp.153-4.

his respects. The visit, a report of which was printed in the Surrealist review *Littérature*,[2] resulted only in Breton's disenchantment. Freud appears to have been living in a remote district of Vienna, and when Breton eventually found him he was confronted by a little, wizened old man who remained very much aloof. Finally, when Breton (who also held a medical degree and had had a good deal of practice in psychiatric wards during the war) happened to mention the names of famous Frenchmen such as Charcot and Babinski, there was no response whatever. All he was told was that he had written 'such a moving letter' and that 'psychoanalysis expected much of the young'.[3]

This was not exactly overwhelming – even if the conversation is certain to have been hampered by Freud's lack of fluency in French and Breton's almost non-existent German. Breton in fact knew Freud's early work only in French translation. Besides, quite apart from the generation gap, there was the *gaffe* unwittingly committed by a Breton ignorant of the extent to which Freud was avid of recognition – particularly for his complete originality. The names of precursors, in this case great teachers of his, such as Charcot, could not have been received with equanimity. Ten years later, in an exchange of letters, Breton even went so far as by implication to accuse Freud of plagiarism in the matter of the symbolic interpretation of dreams; after all, in his bibliographies there was not a single predecessor to be found.[4] Freud thereupon wrote three letters in which he tried to explain. Breton, on his side, added an appendix to his *Vases communicants* of 1932, with a reply addressed 'To the reader'. In his reply he observed that he had evidently touched on a tender spot, and reproached Freud with bourgeois reticence in the concluding pages of his rightly famous self-analysis. But this was not in any way to diminish his admiration.

A further passage from the second manifesto is again particularly enlightening.[5] For attention is there drawn to the ever-increasing importance attached by Freud to censorship on the part of the super-ego. To the Surrealists – that is to say, to Breton – Freud's attitude was sufficient to make them declare that they intended to

[2] Later published in *Les Pas Perdus* (Paris, 1924).
[3] *Les Pas Perdus*, pp.117, 118.
[4] Cf. *Les vases communicants* (Paris, 1981), pp.18f., 173f.
[5] *Les vases communicants*, p.170.

take an entirely different course and would have no truck with such ideas. It is interesting to trace the background of so outspoken an attitude. Freud, it is true, had declared in *The Ego and the Id* that the super-ego was not an ethical tribunal. Yet it is extremely likely that the Surrealists had none the less read this meaning into the concept. Breton's statement therefore affords one more indication of both the respect and the distance maintained by Surrealism vis-à-vis psychoanalysis, and of an undeniable insecurity within their ranks.

Their attitude did not however extend to the few pronouncements made by Freud on modernist movements in art. When asked by Ernest Jones for his opinion of early Dadaism in Zurich he is recorded to have replied, 'it is too idiotic for any decent insanity!' On the other hand, in his last letter to Breton about the alleged plagiarism, we find him recalling that he had received many reports of the interest shown by Surrealists in his work – but also that he had been unable to visualize what exactly Surrealism was.[6] Yet in the last year of the life of the by then world-famous psychiatrist everything changed. Through the mediation of Stephan Zweig (who was also present during the interview), he was visited by a young painter who made a deep impression on him. Indeed, so profound was this impression that in a letter to Zweig of July 1938 he wrote 'I really have reason to thank you for the introduction which brought me yesterday's visitors. For until then I was inclined to look upon Surrealists, who have apparently chosen me for their patron saint, as absolute (let us say 95 per cent, like alcohol) cranks. The young Spaniard, however, with his candid, fanatical eyes and undeniable technical mastery, has made me reconsider my opinion'.[7] This young Spaniard was none other than Salvador Dali, who was at the time already one of the most extravagant of Surrealists.[8]

It is not very likely that Freud had ever seen a work by Dali. And

[6] Cf. Ernest Jones, *Sigmund Freud: Life and Work* (London, 1953-7), 2.44, and *Les vases communicants*, p.176.

[7] 20 July 1938, Freud, *Briefe, 1873-1939*, ed. Ernst L. Freud (Frankfurt am Main, 1960), p.441. Quoted from *Letters of Sigmund Freud, 1873-1939*, translated by Tania and James Stern (London, 1961), p.444.

[8] Dali had signed the congratulatory address for Freud's 80th birthday. During his visit he made a sketch of Freud – cf. Ernest Jones *et al.*, *Sigmund Freud* (New York and London, 1978), p.298 – and he maintained that Freud's cranium was reminiscent of a snail. Cf. Jones, *Freud: Life and Work*, 3.250. At that time there was already friction between Dali and the Surrealists.

he was certainly not aware of the remarkable results obtained by the 'méthode paranoïaque-critique', as Dali had called it. It is hard to believe that Freud could have regarded the bizarre (but also terrifying) associations which were typical of this 'critique' as a serious contribution to knowledge. We must, however, desist from hypothesis. What seems certain is that although Freud may have had an eye for his visitor's technical mastery, he appears above all to have been fascinated by the young man's personality, and to have been perfectly happy to disregard the nature of his work. This, as we have learned, was in keeping with his response to the arts generally. After all, it would seem permissible (and perhaps even essential) that a great genius should have some 'blind spots'.

The Surrealists, for their part, used psychoanalysis to clarify their own intentions and to help achieve them; they borrowed from Freud whatever suited their purpose in whichever form they thought fit. They never claimed to offer an objective, scientific contribution to psychology. What they were deeply convinced of, rather, was that their ideas were more profound than any that science had been able to produce. It is perfectly understandable that they did not feel the urge to follow up the technical elaboration of psychoanalysis down to the last detail and faithfully to register its evolution. A striking illustration of this is provided by a curious failing on their part. It concerns Jung. Precisely where they deviated most markedly from Freud by getting involved at an early stage in all kinds of esoteric doctrines – in occultism, parapsychology and the like – they could have been expected to resort to Jung. But as far as can be ascertained, that never happened.[9] We may be even more surprised when we recall the fundamental importance to psychoanalysis of what Freud called the primary processes – condensation, displacement and symbolization. The Surrealists were certainly very much aware of these concepts; they availed themselves of them in both their literature and their art. But in the theoretical pieces they published there is, however, not a single reference to any of them. Yet once the primary processes had been mentioned, the secondary ones, which had to do with waking thought, inevitably had to be considered as well. For Freud, both in analysis and in therapy, it was always a matter of translating the first category into the second,

[9] Cf. Jean Starobinski, *La relation critique* (Paris, 1970), pp.320f.

because of their very contrast. The Surrealists did not accept such procedures; they wished to abolish antinomies – although, at the same time, they refused to become submerged with Jung in any deep mysticism where the frontiers between dreams or hallucinations and those of waking thought would melt away. It was inevitable that such an aim could only be attained by paradoxical means. Freud wished to get to know the dreams of his patients and to establish systematically what they really meant. The Surrealists went out of their way to live their dreams and to make them available to others in order that they could live them too.

An example of this is to be found in a piece by Paul Eluard of 1930, written in collaboration with Breton and entitled *L'Immaculé conception*. It contains – as apparent from a number of chapter-headings – a consistent attempt at simulating mental debility, psychotic mania, dementia praecox, and so on. And if this indicates the impression meant to be created, even more significant is the outline of the book's programme which, as a chapter called 'Les possessions', is not placed at the opening, and differs from the other chapters only in its typography. The two authors state plainly that poetic minds should be expected to be able to produce delirious ideas consciously and at will. The notion becomes more arresting when we read that their spiritual balance should remain unimpaired and their 'insanity' prove merely temporary. This also does away with the presumptive categories in which those who have a score to settle with human reason are placed.[10]

I may of course prove to have been the victim of a deliberate mystification – or possibly of an unconscious one. Nevertheless, I am inclined to confess a certain susceptibility to such strange and morbidly fascinating principles. The point, at any rate, of referring to this work is to emphasize not its literary significance but the influence of psychiatry, and especially of psychoanalysis, and the remarkable twist given to both at the hands of some Surrealists. That, moreover, is why it is difficult to agree with Edward Glover's indictment of Surrealism as 'ill-digested psychological information'.[11] Perhaps the Surrealists misunderstood psychoanalysis, but they are certain to have digested a good deal of it after their own

[10] Cf. Paul Eluard, *Oeuvres complètes* (Paris, 1968), I.315.
[11] *Freud or Jung* (London, 1950), p.13.

fashion and to have absorbed it into their flesh and blood.

Freud, the analysts, and the Surrealists each went their own way. They did not share a starting-point, nor did they intend to reach the same destination. But this did not prevent their paths crossing repeatedly right from the very beginning. With the global diffusion of both psychoanalysis and Surrealism such encounters became more and more numerous. Indeed, they have been so frequent and often so unexpected that it is hardly feasible to decide at certain points whether it is the one or the other that prevailed. Which is, of course, proof of the untold possibilities inherent in both.

It would be tempting now to consider each occasion on which their paths crossed. But further comment must be limited to two phenomena – automatic writing and aesthetic strangeness. The term 'écriture automatique' denotes a key concept for Surrealism and at once recalls, not Freud but a book entitled *L'Automatisme psychologique*, published in 1889 and written by Pierre Janet – who belonged to the abhorred species of official psychiatrists and who for years had been a leading figure in the field.[12] It is hard to say whether the similarity was coincidental. But our understanding of what the Surrealists had in mind is not hampered by that, for they pronounced more than once on the subject in their own name. Of their many accounts of automatic writing that have come down to us, one is so widely known that it threatens to falsify our perspective. According to this account – which is, indeed, a clear and well-formulated description – automatic writing is at the heart of the Surrealist endeavour, which aspires to pure mental automatism wherein the true and real functioning of the thinking process finds expression. Surrealism therefore expresses what goes on in the mind irrespective of any control exercised by reason or by aesthetic and moral preoccupations.[13] This had already been stated as early as 1924 in the first manifesto, and is such an easily handled formula that everybody was prepared to accept it at its face-value and to take it as an axiom. In its negative implications this course is perfectly correct: moral, religious, or logical restrictions were to be scorned –

[12] On the history of the relations between Freud and Janet see Henri F. Ellenberger, *The Discovery of the Unconscious* (London, 1970), and the interesting criticism of this book by K.R. Eissler, *Talent and Genius* (New York, 1971), pp.342f.

[13] Breton, *Manifestes*, p.40.

aesthetic ones too. The Surrealists' ambition was to achieve an utterly passive and receptive state – 'l'état le plus passif, ou réceptif' – when undertaking to produce a work of art. And it is evident that in putting it this way they thereby enunciated anew the age-old theory of inspiration. But in doing so they went well beyond what had been the accepted norm – while at the same time (*mirabile dictu*, one might say) they were more consistent and more exclusive than practically any of their predecessors.

So far so good; but the question remains of how the Surrealists proposed to set about their task. How were they to take into account the fact that they were not expected to take anything into account? How was it possible to demand complete liberty of artistic expression while at the same time proffering suggestions about how to achieve it? That such contradictions and paradoxes were inevitable did not at first worry the Surrealists unduly. Later, however, when texts produced according to the rules of automatic writing proved to be only too easily imitated and parodied, without having any intrinsic worth, they went back on their tenets.[14] First, the central function accorded to 'écriture automatique' gradually diminished over the years. We find next an increasingly open and regular admittance that aesthetic considerations were to some extent indispensable, although any other considerations remained anathema. And, finally, totally automatic writing was turned into a lofty ideal, into an end religiously to be sought but in fact unattainable, a state of artistic grace as Breton put it, available only to few. One cannot help wondering whether this was not the standard by which to measure the very first products of automatic writing. They could have rated as attempts to achieve an ideal, not as embodiments of it.[15] But even then, the Surrealists would surely have insisted that it had always been their intention to amalgamate apparent contradictions into a higher unity – contradictions which had only been deemed such by an outmoded logic.

It seems almost inconceivable that the utterly unrestrained

[14] Cf. Louis Aragon, *Traité du style* (Paris, 1928), pp.188-9.

[15] Cf. Breton, *Manifestes*, pp.189f., *Entretiens* (Paris, 1952), pp.71f., and *Arcane 17* (Paris, 1947), p. 203. Relapsed Surrealists but permanent admirers of Breton like Caillois and Etiemble rejected 'écriture automatique' and were inclined to consider it as a mystification. Cf. 'André Breton et le mouvement surréaliste', *Nouvelle revue française*, April 1967, pp.688f. and 843.

dictation that was to be supplied by the genuine unconscious should not have recalled Freud's 'free association'. When exactly the phenomenon denoted by the term and the use made of it in therapy were first established is difficult to ascertain. Freud originally based his psychiatric practice on hypnosis. But the difficulties he experienced, and especially the consequence of his impressive self-analysis (in which the discovery of the dream-element helped to explain a great deal), drove Freud to reject hypnosis as a method on principle. As early as his study of hysteria of 1895, a patient's own activity was considered of paramount importance. Free association proved more and more valuable; and the couch in Freud's consulting room, on which his patients could stretch out in order to speak freely and unhindered, has become a world-famous piece of furniture and the very symbol of psychoanalysis.

We need not now dwell on the problem that a patient's free association may be impeded by repression and resistance, and that the analyst has to be aware of various symptoms of these and of the way to overcome them. What concerns us is only that the method of the analyst consists primarily in allowing the patient to speak without guidance, but at the same time in seeing to it that all kinds of defence mechanisms are eliminated. In many respects, therefore, the process exactly resembles what Surrealism was aiming at in its automatic writing.

In his *Psychopathology of Everyday Life* Freud relates how an acquaintance on one of his holidays wanted at a given moment to quote a line from Virgil but succeeded only in part. Having been prompted by Freud, the man was highly irritated by his stupid forgetfulness and asked how this could have happened. Had not Freud always claimed that such a thing would never occur without good reason? Freud accepted the challenge to explain it on condition that he would be told honestly and without prior selection whatever entered the mind of this acquaintance when thinking of the word that had escaped him.[16] The outcome is irrelevant. What matters is to see the parallel with the Surrealists's methods, a parallelism beautifully evidenced in the identical terms they used.

However, from another angle, this similarity is deceptive. The difference resides in the fact that, with psychoanalysis, the word that

[16] *SE*, 6.9.

had been forgotten served as a starting-point, and was decisive, for the conversation that followed. In his *Introductory Lectures on Psycho-Analysis* Freud was subsequently to state that one was free to associate ideas, but only as long as one kept to the initial notion.[17] This is what the Surrealists utterly refused to do. To them such a restriction was repressive – a direct assault on the freedom of the spirit, which they saw as fundamental and essential. What at first sight may have looked like concurrence thus turns out to have been no more than a meeting and dividing of paths. The ideas of Surrealism and psychoanalysis may have had their points of contact, but they functioned in entirely different contexts.

Perhaps the difference is best gauged by looking at the exact value of the term 'free' in the phrase free association. In his *Outline of Psycho-Analysis* Freud explicitly declared that a so-called free association was not really 'free' at all. Once conscious thought had been (as far as possible) eliminated, free associations that emerged were determined by the unconscious material concerned.[18] In spite of all its bizarre variety, therefore, a specific regularity, order, and conformity to certain rules would forthwith become apparent in the process of association, no matter how unusual these rules might seem.

Superficially, the Surrealists did not strike the world as caring greatly about such conformity in their strange products. Their aim, it could be said, was art: Freud's was science. Freud in fact stood for a strict positivism, and a determinism that did not allow of inner contradictions. It is undeniable, however, that over the years psychoanalysis has repeatedly been reproached with being a non-science. One of the reasons for that may be not only the recurrent emphasis laid by Freud and his followers on the 'art of interpretation', but also their constant and significant debt to literature. Freud himself, for example, observed that the theory of free association had been formulated as early as 1823 by Ludwig Börne. Börne was alleged to have declared that should any aspiring writer wish to achieve originality in three days, all he needed to do was to cover the paper uninterruptedly with anything that entered his

[17] *SE*, 15.106.
[18] *SE*, 19.195.

head while studiously avoiding falsification or dissembling.[19] Here is another instance, therefore, of free association being treated as the true authenticity – although the association was of course to be based on insight and tact, in order that a genuine causality might be revealed.

None of this is to be found with the Surrealists. It was not, of course, that they claimed no scientific significance whatever for their activities.[20] They admitted that the direct rendering of a dream would not automatically produce a work of art. But they persisted in seeing the value of their 'écriture automatique' in, among other things, a deep-seated 'knowing' rather than scientific knowledge. They sought a higher or more profound knowledge that went beyond anything traditional science could ever be expected to attain. We are familiar with the fundamental value Freud always attached to reality – a reality which must be known and explored to its very limits. For the Surrealists there were no such limits, only an unfathomable abyss. For them reality was suffused with supernatural phenomena; the wish to establish a separation, or even merely a distinction, between reality and 'surreality' was considered utterly ridiculous. Accordingly, they could not but produce works of art which are still, in the eyes of many, arresting, weird, or indeed downright absurd.

The astonishment registered by readers of Surrealist writings or viewers of Surrealist exhibitions is, of course, a result of the aesthetic strangeness with which they find themselves confronted. This is not merely caused by facing the unexpected and unaccustomed. For centuries artists have always (up to a point) banked on upsetting their audience or the general public by producing truly novel works. What was new was an essential 'strangeness on principle' – which, since the 1920s, we have become increasingly used to. If the glass tumbler of Marcel Duchamp could rank as a form of Dadaist anti-art, intent on undermining traditional values and notions in order to dethrone official art from within, the artists' aim soon enough shifted towards

[19] *SE*, 18.265. I should be tempted to see in it an ironical mystification, but Freud seems to be convinced. Freud also mentions his admiration for Börne in his youth, but writes that he did not remember these lines, which were communicated to him by his friend and disciple Ferenczi on the suggestion of a third person.

[20] It is interesting to note that Lacan, who considered himself the new Freud, had frequented Surrealist circles and was befriended by Salvador Dali.

providing their tumblers with an entirely novel content. It was pure chance – and games – that acquired a central significance in Surrealist works.

In collective performances the early representatives of Surrealism did all sorts of things which we should be inclined to see as parlour games. They would write down quite arbitrarily a little sentence on a scrap of paper, which was then folded and handed to the next person who, in turn, would jot down whatever entered his head, and so on. The outcome was, if not a work of art, at any rate an illustration of what could be achieved by allowing chance to take its course. And it is true that occasionally, thanks to this 'hasard objectif', pieces of writing emerged which were curious and sometimes moving. Similarly, in exhibitions of 'objets surréalistes' – 'collages', 'frottages', and so on – chance had, as it were, been challenged and had been allowed to have its own way. Although the guidance of chance was never total (the exhibits undoubtedly displaying a certain *arrangement*) there thus originated what we have come to recognize nowadays as objects which are no objects, the so-called 'objets fantômes', the mysterious pictures of incomprehensible but none the less impressive dreams or the senseless yet still oddly fascinating poetry.[21]

Some will not hesitate, if only in a whisper, to agree with Freud's phrase: 'too idiotic for decent insanity'. Such an attitude is not wholly justified, however. What the Surrealists hoped to achieve in proceeding so 'strangely' was not simply the result of a conscious and reprehensible desire to shock by presenting the unknown and the unexpected. They wanted, first of all, to show that our everyday experience is unique and miraculous, just as the seemingly miraculous and exceptional is part of this everyday experience and should be recognized as such. At any moment, and in anyone's life, inconceivable occurrences will take place – occurrences which André Breton called 'pétrifiantes coincidences', and which we are all familiar with. One walks down the street and happens to think of somebody who years before used to be a close acquaintance. And within five minutes one is facing him. For most of us this is pure coincidence. Not so for the Surrealists. While certainly not invoking

[21] Cf. Breton, *Le Surréalisme et la peinture* (Paris, 1965), and *Manifestes*, p.305, where he refers in this context to Hegel.

divine providence, they had always considered such occurrences to be fundamental elements of human existence, and accordingly endeavoured to make use of them. That is why they undertook to provoke such phenomena and to systematize their provocation. In this respect, too, one of Breton's first works, *Nadja*, remains a prototype. In it, a sense of the supernatural and the marvellous which influences everyday reality in an almost magical way goes hand in hand with ecstasy, fear and horror.

When the strangeness of everyday experience is concerned, this is hardly astonishing; with the help of Freud's approach, it might even have proved the more readily understandable. In 1919 Freud had published *The Uncanny* – the English title being a translation of the German *Das Unheimliche*, for which 'disconcerting' or 'upsetting' would have done as well, or even better. By these three terms, at any rate, practically all aspects of the marvellous are alluded to – with one exception. As usual, Freud set out by offering a fairly lengthy etymological exposition. It is as if the term was by itself to underpin his argument about the phenomenon. The German adjective *heimlich* is liable to interpretation in two different ways. Both are naturally derived from *Heim* – English 'home'. But one interpretation of *heimlich* would tend towards the English 'cosy' or 'homely', the other towards the English 'secret' or even 'secretive'. The latter sense is the exact opposite of the former. Freud emphatically pointed to the feelings of dread and horror associated with the uncanny, and offered a host of instances, culled almost without exception from literature – to the inclusion even of the motif of the *Doppelgänger*, the 'double'. What his semantic analysis boiled down to was that uncanny situations originate in repressed fears, in which those of castration and death play a prominent part, side by side with unconscious desires. In addition, Freud showed that much of what would have been experienced as uncanny in everyday life was not presented as such in literature. For Freud, any experience of the uncanny was always a re-living of infantile anxieties – as in the case of the demoniacal forces embodied in ghosts and apparitions – and therefore a form of superstition and, in a sense, of regression. The truly mature adult would not give in to this and would remain focused on reality. In this context, too, art presented a vehicle for the mild expression of unconscious fears, rendering them supportable and even agreeable.

Once again the Surrealists' position reveals parallels with, and differences from, Freudian theory. They did not apparently concern themselves with the theory of the complexes Freud was dealing with, although they cannot have been unaware of them, those of fear and horror in particular. For the Surrealists, however, repression was as unthinkable as an art which, by inducing gratuitous shudders, merely lures the reader towards existing complexes. They would on the contrary go out of their way to present these complexes as starkly as possible, and thereby, precisely, to master them. As indicated earlier on, they were playing a serious – and dangerous – game of simulation. Their art was therefore a form which surrendered to unknown forces, and which as a result could only be upsetting and disconcerting. Viewers of Surrealist paintings in the early years will have visited an exhibition with some expectation of what a picture ought to look like. Consciously or unconsciously they would have at once applied a set of rules they had been equipped with. Any work of art that did not conform to these rules was upsetting: whatever was not in concert with the trusted and familiar, and therefore with the artistically pleasing, was disconcerting.

In retrospect it would not, however, seem that Surrealism had done anything startlingly new by breaking certain patterns of behaviour. But what was innovatory was the force applied in doing so, and (unforeseen, and probably also unwanted, by Freud) the way in which the unconscious and dreams were brought into the open. The uncanny was given a decidedly positive value, a colour of its own, and a hardly innocuous, but, rather, terrifying beauty.

Now so far as therapy is concerned, psychoanalysis may well be regarded as a means of overcoming the difficulties and tensions with which we have to contend in our struggle with reality and our struggle for mastery of the self. Humour can also be regarded in this light. In his *Jokes and their Relation to the Unconscious*, Freud focused his attention on the funny, comic and amusing. In practically all its forms, humour was proved to be an expression of aggressiveness and often to consist in unexpected connections of disparate ideas. Humour as such, furthermore, was presented as being a defence against 'unpleasure'. Are we therefore justified in assuming that humour is a guilty – and at the same time innocent – form of resistance against, and, in a sense, a flight from, reality and its inherent dangers? (Guilty, because the true struggle with reality – which is, after all, what matters – is never engaged; innocent because the aggression is never acted out and actually remains merely verbal.) However, viewed from either angle humour offers a chance to regard oneself as an outsider would, and in this way to see the other person within, and possibly also to see what the otherness consists in. This is what the Surrealists were alive to; they were always as a matter of course sensitive to the strange and the absurd. But the anthology of literary humorists, which Breton published in 1950, was called *Anthologie de l'humour noir*, and the 'noir' was not irrelevant. To Freud, humour was a kind of battle, or at least a line of defence; the Surrealists, in contrast, added, as it were, an extra dimension. To them there was no humour that was not essentially black humour. Even if we no longer pay much attention to the old humour theories, the black bile of the melancholy humour is still an indispensable element in our conception. Humour never occurs but 'sur le fond du désespoir', as Breton had it; and no joke is conceivable but at one remove from despair. Freud is inevitably referred to in Breton's anthology: at the same time his notions are not taken over without some basic adjustments. First, we are not so much to think of a struggle with reality as of its total rejection. For the early Surrealists, any notion of reality was merely ludicrous and, up to a point, utterly useless. The dangers inherent in reality were not combated by humour but absorbed in it. They only constituted its background and basis. Yet again, therefore, we find a crossing of paths – and a rapid subsequent divergence.

In what has been said so far we have only scratched the surface of a very large area. Of the various and unavoidable omissions, however, there is one which must be repaired, no matter how superficially. For the impression may have been created that the history of psychoanalysis and Surrealism has a bearing on only modern literature and art. In his essay *Of Beauty* Bacon wrote: 'there is no excellent beauty that hath not some strangeness in the proportion'. True, this was said in connection with the doctrine of proportion, but 'strangeness' is his starting-point; and a few centuries later Edgar Allan Poe was to quote this particular statement out of preference – a preference which, for Baudelaire and for Aestheticism, became a matter of unshakable principle.[22] In a sense, the uncanny

[22] Cf. *Strangeness and Beauty: An Anthology of Aesthetic Criticism 1840-1910*, ed. Eric Warner and Graham Hough, 2 vols (Cambridge, 1983). It would not be difficult to find numerous earlier references; I mention only Vasari's epitaph for Piero di Cosimo in the first edition of his *Vite* and Hippolyta's words in Shakespeare's *Midsummer Night's Dream*, act 5 scene 1, lines 25-7.

has never been absent from art. And the uncanny naturally involves the horrific. Ever since Aristotle there has been no lack of a sense of dread and terror in literature. Nor must we overlook the 'terribilità' which has so often been praised and rejected in Michelangelo. In what other context, moreover, do Piranesi's *Carceri* fit so easily? The fact that such examples do not at once present themselves is simply the result of getting accustomed to them. For each may very well be compared to what the Surrealists endeavoured. One could even go so far as to hold that in the end it was Freud and the Surrealists who together opened our eyes to the uncanny and marvellous in the past, and turned them into an integral part of the present. Accordingly, it is not hard to discover Surrealist elements in Petronius's *Cena Trimalchionis*, or at Burgundian banquets in the late Middle Ages and in the stately ballets devised for royal entertainment in the sixteenth and seventeenth centuries. But there was one great difference: the enormous pies that disgorged enchanting musicians were certainly strange but never terrifying. They served for amusement and relaxation. Their strangeness was fleeting and never aspired to promote any deep sense of the nature of human existence.

So much for the uncanny. Is it conceivable that the same can be said of the aesthetics of chance? For an answer we need only recall that, side by side with the ancient and venerable tradition of conscious and practised professional skill, based on the strict observance of rules, there existed a no less ancient and venerable tradition emphasizing the importance of sudden and unexpected inspiration: the artist was incited to create beyond his own volition, indeed beyond his actual awareness. What is more, in his *Natural History* Pliny relates the amusing story of the painter Protogenes who, in spite of his considerable technical skill, was unable convincingly to render the foam of a panting dog. His picture bespoke great ability but was not sufficiently natural. He finally fell into a rage and dashed a sponge against the offending spot in the picture – and chance produced the effect of nature in the painting. When we recollect that the books of so revered a classical author were read and re-read in the Renaissance, the possible impact of this text will be clear at once.[23] One may assume that the Surrealists would have

[23] Book 35: 36, 102-3. Cf. H.W. Janson, 'The "Image made by chance" in Renaissance thought', in his *Sixteen Studies* (New York, 1973), pp.53-74.

appreciated this story; they would surely have found in it an example of the impenetrable mystery of creativity. Freud, on the other hand, would have interpreted the story as presenting an enigma completely determined by the unconscious and thereby, albeit with great pains, eventually to be solved.

It is time to put an end to these historical excursions – although to Surrealists, who hold with 'poésie interrompue' in life and letters, a real ending does not exist. Freud was partial to endings, and it may well for him have been a symbolic act that, whenever he had concluded a study or an article, he would destroy both notes and manuscript. Of course, many further parallels and contrasts between Surrealism and psychoanalysis can be adduced. The links between the two were possibly based on mutual misunderstanding, and certainly on a time lag. When in 1924 the French Surrealists gathered around the first manifesto, they based themselves among other things on Freud's writings of twenty-five years before. But Freud happened to have changed his ideas radically in his metapsychology of the 1920s. *The Ego and the Id* of 1923 is a case in point. As far as can be ascertained, the Surrealists took no notice of this evolution.

The id – the Latin translation of the German *Es* – was to be regarded as a tank of energy, replenished by the primary instincts; the ego was the most important 'constant' in the life of the spirit. The point, then, is that the ego integrates the id as much as possible and eventually takes its place. Freud actually said so in a later work, the *New Introductory Lectures*: 'wo Es war, soll Ich werden' ('where id was there ego shall be'). And he added (a Dutchman is delighted to quote) that this was a cultural achievement comparable only to the draining of the Zuiderzee.[24] The Surrealists would not have agreed with this at all. For whereas Freud's point of departure was that the id must be absorbed and overcome by the ego, Surrealism wished to go in the opposite direction: while keeping the ego intact, they paradoxically wanted it to be submerged in the id. Here again, therefore, Surrealism and psychoanalysis met – but to part company at once. It is fortunate that they did not really clash.

All we can do in the present context, then, is to offer confirmation of previous suggestions – that there may have been misunderstand-

[24] *SE*, 22.80.

ing on both sides. If so, however, it was surely one of those felicitous and fertile misunderstandings to which, over the centuries, European civilization has owed so much.

CHAPTER SIX

Psychoanalysis and Anthropology

Francis Huxley

It is now sixty-five years since psychoanalysis made its first advances to anthropology, between the covers of Freud's *Totem and Taboo*. Reactions were varied, as they still are. In some quarters the suitor was treated with respect, and turned down only when his contractual terms proved unsuitable; elsewhere he was suspected of attempting a marriage by capture, and the assembled kin took pleasure in beating him off. Here and there the flirtation ended in common-law marriages, one or two of which have stood the test of time; but one cannot say that the union has ever been properly sanctified.

On the face of it, the match was a very suitable one. At the time, both psychoanalysis and anthropology were evolutionarily minded, and assumed the psychic unity of mankind; also they shared large interests in magic, in religion, incest, exogamy, sacrifice, sacred kings and, of course, in totems and taboos. There were, however, some patent inequalities between their positions, for if Freud spoke for psychoanalysis with his own voice, anthropology had to speak with many. It was, for instance, still arguing over the evolution of marriage: had there at one time been a state of promiscuity followed by fourteen evolutionary stages from group marriage, the consanguineous family, polygamy, to monogamy? Or was monogamy the primal stage? What of primitive matriarchy? And what on earth was the incest taboo about?

For all these problems Freud had an answer, and the answers fitted into a single story. He had been noting the problems in his own practice, and found the anthropological evidence confirmed his solution perfectly, even if he had to take it from disparate sources. From Darwin he took the evolutionary hypothesis and the notion of the primitive horde; from Atkinson, the plot of the murder of the primal father; from Robertson Smith the nature of the totemic feast; and from Tylor, Marett and, most of all, from Frazer, ethnological accounts and opinions. It is worth remembering that Malinowski praised the empirical fecundity of this work for anthropological research, and of *The Golden Bough*, whose erudition and charm also captivated a much larger audience. There, as A.E. Housman declared in his 'Address to Sir James Frazer', readers find 'learning mated with literature, labour disguised in ease, and a museum of dark and uncouth superstitions invested with the charm of a truly sympathetic magic. There you have gathered together, for the admonition of a proud and oblivious race, the scattered and fading relics of its foolish childhood, whether withdrawn from our view among savage folk, or lying unnoticed at our doors'.[1] We shall not expect to see again such a palatial ordering of pagan memorabilia, commented on with such noble – if often misleading – common sense: the kind which Radcliffe-Brown took exception to, when he remarked that Frazer explained things on the 'if I were a horse' principle.

Let us remember what Frazer was doing. He believed firmly in evolution, but was all the same not exactly Darwinian, for he made nothing of the doctrine of natural selection. None the less he was a materialist in the Darwinian style in that he translated structure into habit and thus into function – though the habits he was interested in were all ritual.

These rituals, though many and disparate, had yet something in common with each other; indeed, it seemed that there was a large ritual form in which they were once embodied, here known as totemism, there as sacred kingship, while the form of these forms was the universal pattern, the life and death of the incarnate deity.

He proved the logic of this construction by examining a great number of strange things, and his sober interest in what he called the venerable antics of mankind never flagged. To read him aright one does well to remember that he worked twelve hours a day for

[1] Quoted in R. Angus Downie, *Sir James Frazer and the Golden Bough* (London, 1970), p.28.

sixty years without intermission, as his friend Angus Downie said, not driven by some daemonic drive of conscience but labouring patiently with the constitution of one of the great grammarians of his day.[2] If one can follow him with equal pace one sees the body of this incarnate deity pieced together like Osiris, from fragments scattered over the globe – fragments picked up from peasants in Europe or China, among Malays or Dyaks, the eastern Indians of North America or the Szis of Upper Burma, from the Middle East, India, or classical antiquity – and taking shape as a ritual organism of worldwide proportions.

True, Frazer makes one believe that these things happen far away or long ago. His evolutionary scheme goes from magic, which is how savages do things, to religion, which the Comparative Method will soon put to flight, to Science, in whose light we should all now comport ourselves; so that if he warns the reader of the universal body of savagery to be found beneath the surface of civilization, he remains confident that reason can overcome it. It is thus with no sense of alarm that he can write:

> It is indeed a melancholy and in some respects a thankless task to strike at the foundations of beliefs in which, as in a strong tower, the hopes and aspirations of humanity throughout long ages have sought a refuge from the storm and stress of life. Yet sooner or later it is inevitable that the battery of the comparative method should breach these venerable walls, mantled over with the ivy and mosses and wild flowers of a thousand tender and sacred associations. At present we are only dragging the guns into position: they have hardly begun to speak.[3]

It is within such venerable walls that one must picture Frazer writing these words, and on another occasion receiving a visitor with intelligence from the Dyaks. He was told, Angus Downie recounts, that when a child is born, the Dyak father holds his head so that any blood shed should drip on it; whereupon Frazer said, 'I never realized that blood could be shed at childbirth'.[4] Nor could this type of an eighteenth-century gentleman, as Downie describes him,

[2] Downie, p.21.
[3] *The Golden Bough*, ed. T.H. Gaster (New York, 1959), p.xxvi.
[4] Downie, p.19.

realize that the big guns he had in mind were soon to turn into phallic symbols, and that once religion was destroyed, the universal body of savagery beneath civilization would appear on the psychoanalyst's couch.

When he read what was afoot in *Totem and Taboo*, he therefore acknowledged neither Freud's offering nor his letter accompanying it, and in the five years that followed was heard to mention its author but once – 'that creature Freud', he said, and left it at that.[5] This was one of the many occasions when it must have been borne in on Freud that he was, as Ernest Jones said of him, no judge of men.[6] It is alarming to see how many of his followers killed themselves, defected, or were expelled as heretics: Tausk, Silberer, Abraham, Rank, Jung, Reich, Adler, even that sweetest of minds, Ferenczi. Nor, apparently, was psychoanalysis any better at judging: Abram Kardiner tells of a man who expressed a great disappointment with his friend who did something unexpected. In complaining to Freud he said, 'well, I guess you don't know anything about anybody until you analyse them'. Freud replied, 'and what do you know then?'[7]

The dissimilarity between these two men went deep. Frazer was never so happy as when he was planting his evolutionary and totemic tree in an agricultural setting – which Malinowski complimented him for. But he did push things, so that Andrew Lang had to twit him in a review for over-exercising the Vegetation deity, and this put Frazer into quite a deep depression.[8] Freud, on the other hand, had come fresh from the hunt after animal phobias, and was quite certain that the deity was one of flesh and blood: also that it committed incest, killed its own father, and would put out its own eyes if it could not put out those of its rivals. Moreover it was infantile and very little conscious of what it was up to: and it was gifted with a conscience bad enough to make its utterances highly ambivalent.

In demonstrating these matters Freud's method was Frazerian enough: he too referred his material to a ritual origin, the Oedipus complex. He turned to anthropology in order to validate its status first as a universal then as *the* universal: which entailed giving it an

[5] Downie, p.21.

[6] Vincent Brome, *Ernest Jones* (London, 1982), p.77.

[7] In *Culture and Personality*, ed. S. Stansfield Sargeant and Marian W. Smith (New York, 1949), p.91.

[8] Downie, p.44.

origin myth. Imagine, then, the primal horde ruled by a jealous and tyrannical father, whose sons are his frustrated and angry rivals. The sons kill the father and glut their revenge with a cannibal feast: an indigestible remorse sets in which causes them to give up their rights in the father's property and go on a search after somebody else's women. After a time this becomes fashionable, and men regularly exchange their women in the shadow of the murdered father, whose death is now totemistically celebrated so that the offence can be safely repeated. In a stroke, then, the story describes the origin of the incest taboo, of exogamy, totemic feasts and purification ceremonies: in a word, of conscience and culture.

If this was the altar at which Freud wished to pledge his troth with anthropology, one can understand why Frazer turned cold all over. I doubt that Darwin would have acted otherwise. Yet Freud was a better Darwinian than Frazer, for he included the psychological analogue of natural selection in his description. Substitute 'libidinal conflicts' for 'the struggle for existence', and you have the gist of the matter: for though one takes place in the economy of nature at large, and the other in the psychic economy, both may yet account for the origin of some definable species. Freud also favoured the Lamarckian theory of inheritance, as Darwin had done at one time, and to this he added Haeckel's biogenetic law, that ontogeny recapitulates phylogeny. This was something of an embarrassment to his later followers, but there was a sound intuition in it all the same, partly because of the importance of the infantile situation in psychoanalysis; and when Róheim replaced the biogenetic law with the idea of fetalization[9] – Gavin de Beer's neoteny[10] – its merits could be appreciated in an ethological as well as a psychoanalytic manner.

But there are two places where Darwin and Freud part company. Darwin was a gradualist both in his ecological and his evolutionary thought: 'poco a poco se anda lejos' might be his motto. But Freud was a catastrophist, as his myth makes clear. What is more, he introduced a most uncomfortable absolute into the works. For, armed in one hand with the inheritance of acquired characteristics, and in the other with the recapitulatory theory of embryology, he could claim that the memory of the primal murder, and of its

[9] Géza Róheim, *Psychoanalysis and Anthropology* (New York, 1950), pp.397f.
[10] Gavin de Beer, *Embryos and Ancestors* (Oxford, 1940).

consequences, is present in every child born thereafter, who must then infallibly repeat the Oedipal process; and if society has anything to do with the matter, it is in terms of anamnesis and not through direct indoctrination. The infantile situation is of course of prime importance in forming the final character, for everyone is different: and societies too differ. But this is merely a historical matter, and in no way affects the universality of the Oedipal mode.

This is one of the capital points in the argument, and Freud's orthodox successors continue to insist upon it.[11] Here they have been joined by the ethologically minded, such as Tiger and Fox,[12] who see culture as the evolutionarily given mode by which the human animal achieves maturity. But Freud had other axes to grind, and was not exactly what passes for a humanist these days. He was rather, as he called himself, an infidel Jew: we find him writing in 1925 that it is not 'perhaps entirely a matter of chance that the first advocate of psychoanalysis was a Jew',[13] with Ferenczi and Reik[14] saying Amen. David Bakan has traced many of the consequences in his book *Sigmund Freud and the Jewish Mystical Tradition*,[15] where he shows the haunting similarity between a psychoanalytic and a Judaic exegesis: and we can appreciate the position for ourselves by noting Freud's choice of anthropological material to support his conclusions. What are the Australian aborigines, with their fierce circumcision rites, their patriarchal leanings, food taboos and exogamous clan practices, but antipodean Semites who await their Moses? One must remember – as Bakan does – that *Totem and Taboo* has a companion volume only published much later – *Moses and Monotheism*, in which the catastrophe that civilized the primal horde is repeated on the slopes of Mount Sinai. It is Moses who now occupies the place of the primal father and who brings down the Tables of the Law from the theophanic din of the Oedipal situation – an anticulinary moment, as Lévi-Strauss would say – for which, according to Freud's tendentious suspicions, he too was murdered. Freud ponders the dreadful problem this raises in front of Michelangelo's great sculpture: he sees in it the super-ego with a

[11] Róheim, p.451.

[12] L. Tiger and R. Rox, *The Imperial Animal* (London, 1971).

[13] *SE*, 19.222.

[14] See Brome, p.109; Theodor Reik, *Ritual: Psycho-Analytic Studies* (London, 1931), pp.23f.

[15] New York, 1958.

human face, divinized with horns and heavy with contained and moralizing rage. Surely it would be better if psychoanalysis were to be seated there, even if it meant committing the ancient crime yet again.

We can ponder this moment ourselves, with Kluckhohn's remarks on occupational psychosis in mind. 'The role of ideological complexes in the formation of anthropological theories,' he writes, 'seems to me to have been (to varying degrees) neglected in almost all of the discussions of anthropological theory which have been published so far.'[16] The same plainly is true of psychoanalytic theories, and of Freud's in particular. We must imagine him listening to the voice from out of the Burning Bush which declared 'I am that I am' as he reformulates the Oedipus complex as the wish of a man to be father to himself: the voice, which is that of *the* Father, triumphs through the castration complex and offers the covenant by which all others must be different, though each has the right also to say 'I am'.

It should be fairly plain by now that if psychoanalysis was the method by which Freud came to such conclusions, the conclusions themselves are in a different category. No longer are we dealing with a psychology, but with an autology. I borrow this word from Coomaraswamy, in his *Hinduism and Buddhism*: following the tradition of the Upanishads he reaches the same general conclusion as Freud, namely that there is a pre-existent self, caught in the toils of ancestral generation and recapitulating its history in every individual; like a Freudian infant, it projects its desires into the outer world, and couples with its reflection in order to stock the world with its fauna and flora, other human beings included; and it constantly sacrifices itself to itself in the hope of becoming One again, with the social order as its forcing-house. And as he describes these matters he writes:

> You must have begun to realize that the theology and the autology are one and the same science, and that the only possible answer to the question 'What am I?' must be 'That art Thou'. For as there are two in him who is both love and death, so there are, as all tradition affirms unanimously, two in us: although not two of him or two of us, nor even one of him and one of us, but only one of both.[17]

[16] Quoted in Róheim, p.459.
[17] A.K. Coomaraswamy, *Hinduism and Buddhism* (New York [1943]), p.15.

For love and death, read Eros and Thanatos: though the low esteem in which Thanatos is held by Freudians today shows their dislike of the autology Freud himself had arrived at, and of having to consider what an autology amounts to. George Devereux indeed remarks that it was only after Freud had postulated the death instinct that he admitted the possibility of telepathy[18] – which, to Devereux, is scientifically (and perhaps morally) questionable. But the autological component in psychoanalysis is central to it for all that, as witness the irritation of many a critic who finds his complaints used as evidence against him to the greater glory of the Freudian scheme.

Now this kind of bad manners is not allowed in scientific circles, which give credence to a proposition only in so far as it allows the facts the chance of disproving the null hypothesis. All the same, Freud must be granted his point. His psychoanalytic universe deals with ego and id, the conscious and the unconscious, with intervening mechanisms to convert the one into the other by means of ambiguity and displacement. This is what symbols are about. The ego has the property of self-reference and the ability to say 'no'; the id that of turning everything into its opposite so that opposites can be reduced to a unity, to such an extent that 'there is nothing in the id that can be compared to negation'.[19] These two sub-systems are complementary and simultaneous, and if the whole tries to use the null hypothesis on itself, the result can only be suicide. The logical demonstration of this can be seen in Gödel's Proof, which showed that if arithmetic – that is, any logical system of notation – is consistent, it is incomplete; with the corollary that if it is complete, it is inconsistent. This is also true of an autology, the grand extension of Russell's paradoxes of self-reference, which can only be solved by installing a hierarchy of meta-statements in the works; which done it is still possible to hold, as Gödel did, that 'classes and concepts may be conceived as real objects existing independently of our definitions and constructions. It seems to me that the assumption of such objects is quite as legitimate as the assumption of physical bodies, and there is quite as much reason to believe in their existence'.[20]

[18] George Devereux, 'The works of George Devereux', in *The Making of Psychological Anthropology*, ed. G.D. Spindler (Berkeley and Los Angeles, 1978), p.396.

[19] See Norman O. Brown, *Life Against Death* (London, 1960), p.320.

[20] Quoted in Ernest Nagel and J.R. Newman, *Gödel's Proof* (London, 1959), p.100.

But Freud was not interested in opening up his autology in this way. What he did was to close it on itself, according to the psychoanalytic method he had perfected: and the result was a double bind, in which Russell and Gödel were helplessly tied up. So of course was Freud, as may be deduced from his reactions before Michelangelo's Moses. Here was the personification of his autology, which his psychoanalysis was hoping to dethrone: but if it succeeded, it would be in the name of the same autology and, once installed, would invite similar attacks. No wonder then that Freud was so jealous to preserve the integrity of his science, and dealt with heretics so severely.

The Freudian bind has two other characteristics worth mentioning. It is, for a start, what makes a complex a complex; and it is by understanding its rules that dreams and symbols can be interpreted so that they conform to the rules. Secondly, it is couched in the accusatory mode: that is, as Róheim said, 'it is good psychoanalytic methodology to try to explain the normal on the basis of the pathological'.[21] Taken together, these explain some of the excesses psychoanalysis is notorious for, as when Ernest Jones psychoanalysed the Holy Ghost and proved it to be nothing but a fantasy caused by infantile flatus.[22] There may be something in what he says, but the brutality of the reduction speaks against it.

It was thus fortunate for everyone when Malinowski, under Seligman's direction, applied 'some of Freud's conclusions directly to savage psychology and customs, while actually engaged in field-work'.[23] He approved of Freud's sociological theory, which accorded with that of Westermarck – and of Malinowski – concerning the antiquity of individual and monogamous marriage, and so scorned the rival theory of primitive promiscuity. But amongst the natives of the Trobriands he found some difficulties in applying the scheme, since there the father was the affectionate friend and helper of his children, the 'ferocious matriarch' being the mother's brother.

Also, the incest taboo was mainly directed towards the separation

[21] Róheim, p.442.

[22] 'A psycho-analytic study of the Holy Ghost', in *Essays in Applied Psycho-Analysis* (London, 1922).

[23] B. Malinowski, letter to *Nature*, 3 November 1923, in *Sex, Culture, and Myth* (London, 1926), p.114.

of brother and sister, though it did divide mother and son too. 'Thus we have a pattern of family life in which the two elements decisive for psychoanalysis, the repressive authority and the severing taboo, are "displaced", disturbed in a manner different from that found in the patriarchal family. If Freud's general theory is correct, there ought to be also a change in the thwarted desires; the repressed wish-formation ought to receive a shape different from the Oedipus complex.'[24]

He also claimed that the Trobrianders showed no sign of the anal complex. Freud had nothing to say about this other than 'what, have they then no anus?'[25] – which is a more thorough refutation than the uninitiated might like to think. As for the other objections, Malinowski himself helped to save the appearances. The repressed wish formations did receive a different shape, and that in a most remarkable confirmation of Freudian theories; indeed they allowed the Functional Anthropologist 'to trace the pattern of instinctive and emotional tendencies in the texture of the social fabric'.[26]

But this satisfied neither the psychoanalysts nor Malinowski's colleagues. On the one hand he was attacked for being quite inadequately informed and plainly anti-psychoanalytical, on the other for treating each culture 'as a closed system except in so far as its elements correspond to vital biological urges',[27] with the family as the fundamental unit in all human society. This last thrust came from the staunch Boasian, Lowie, who, in Weston La Barre's words, 'responded to the meteoric rise of Malinowski with a truly vituperative tone, all the more remarkable in this ordinarily judicial-minded, good gray historian of ethnological science'.[28]

The situation is too complicated to describe now in anything but a caricature. Let us then put it this way: functionalism is the offspring of Frazerian thoughts about the totemic organization and the experience of fieldwork: the ritual organization can be seen to work hand in hand with the organization of the family, and the empirical value of savage institutions can now be appreciated on their own terms. But this achievement necessarily entails a loss of interest in

[24] Malinowski, p.116.
[25] Róheim, p.159.
[26] Malinowski, p.119.
[27] Quoted in Weston La Barre, 'The clinic and the field', in Spindler, p.267.
[28] Spindler, p.267.

the comparative method as it was then being practised, hence Lowie's criticism; and though Freud must have been glad to see anthropology putting ritual and family life together, he must have been dismayed to find that once again his concept of the unconscious was misunderstood. For the Oedipus complex is formed unconsciously, in infancy, and without benefit of sociological role.

Meanwhile, two other developments had occurred. Just at the time when Malinowski's ferocious matriarch, the mother's brother, was making his appearance in anthropology, his sister was being heard saying 'Oedipus shmoedipus, as long as he loves his mother'. She was speaking through Melanie Klein, by then embarked on her long career as the exponent of the good and the bad breast, and of their place in forming the conscience before the father enters the scene. Freud countered by saying that if this were admitted it would mean rewriting the whole Oedipal theory; but that, since he had already thought of the phallic mother (he had thought of everything) and found a place for her in the scheme, his formulation would have to stand.

It was, however, beginning to bulge in a rather unsightly manner; and the birth may be said to have taken place in the United States with the arrival of psychoanalysis on those shores. 'We are bringing them the plague,' as Freud said to Jung. One form of the plague came to be called Culture and Personality Studies, and its explanatory course ran from toilet training to national character, and, as often as not, back again: and its first anthropological victims were Boasian.

Boas at the time was fighting to preserve anthropology from the deterministic claims of the social eugenicists of the day. Here Freud's insistence on the importance of the infantile situation was a most useful ally: with its help one could demonstrate that human nature is infinitely malleable, and that there is no direct influence of genetics on culture. The comparative method had here turned turtle to become the doctrine of cultural relativity, which in turn took on the roseate hues of culture as the superorganic. Culture could now be opposed to Nature in the simplest way, with toilet training and the superorganic combining into a Zeitgeist, which combination could operate the twin theses of the new school: first, that culture is the exclusive determinant of personality; second, that personality consists exclusively in the internalization of culture.

Melford Spiro, whose formulation I have here borrowed, has no difficulty in showing that these theses are not tenable; the simple isomorphism postulated between personality defined as internalized culture, and culture defined as interpersonal behaviour, depends on the assumption that the human organism is an empty or black box with no resilient transformationary powers of its own, which is patently absurd.[29] There is besides, as many others have noted, a chicken and the egg paradox involved in the position, which Freud would wearily have stigmatized as yet another instance of Oedipal thinking, namely the wish to be father of oneself. The theorists were of course aware of this problem, but they hived it off into a separate department of thought called Culture Change: not that they could handle the paradox any better, with some, like Kroeber, excluding individuals as agents of change, and others, like Kluckhohn, disagreeing profoundly.

When Géza Róheim arrived on the scene he had his own criticisms to make. For a start, and with ample psychoanalytic justification, he held that everything depended on conflict, which lies 'not between nature and culture but between the *drive* and the *introject*'. Further, he strongly suspected 'that what we are analysing when we talk about modern nations is the super-ego or ego-ideal of the upper strata, which may or may not be derivable from the infantile situation. The criticism of a young lady in Tokyo about Ruth Benedict's *The Chrysanthemum and the Sword* (1946) is very much to the point. "It sounds like a school-teacher here, speaking to his pupils" '.[30]

Benedict was indeed speaking as a school-teacher, to her fellow Americans at war; so perhaps was Geoffrey Gorer in *The American People*, though more to the prejudices of his own countrymen. Of this work Kluckhohn had to remark that 'statements are made so boldly and are sometimes so flagrantly contradictory to general experience, and to the published literature, that one regrets the publication of this book as an "anthropological and psychoanalytic" study'.[31] But Kluckhohn fared no better at Róheim's hands when he remarked that Navaho children who had no sphincter discipline for their first year and only very gentle discipline thereafter yet emerged with

[29] Melford Spiro, 'Culture and human nature', in Spindler, p.351.
[30] Róheim, pp.452, 387.
[31] Quoted in Róheim, p.366. Cf. Gorer, *The American People* (New York, 1948).

roughly the distortions and fears common to children of every culture, and surmised that psychoanalysis had placed undue emphasis on infant disciplining. This, said Róheim, was no refutation of psychoanalysis but its confirmation. 'Whatever the mother may do or not do,' he answered, 'the child on account of its *own oral aggressions* (Melanie Klein, Bergler, etc.) will project the mother (and later the father) as a cannibal demon.'[32]

George Devereux was later to criticize the obsessionally pragmatic interest in child-rearing techniques by claiming that the ethnic personality was formed not by the techniques but by the mood of the parents when mediating, to the child, through such techniques, the culture of his tribe.[33] Plainly, there are endless refinements to be made to the doctrine, and one should not forget Róheim's demonstration that, as far as an ethnic Hungarian personality was concerned, there was no such thing.[34]

In like manner Kardiner was taken to task for ruling out the element of father-hatred in the Marquesas, and therefore the Oedipus complex, though there might be a mild Electra complex in the works – what pleasure Róheim must have had in adducing the obvious and contradictory evidence.[35] Similarly Erikson was chided for leaving out of his otherwise perceptive account of the Yurok sweat-lodge the conflict element, and for denying the anal complex amongst these people – it was a 'tube complex', he argued. The anal complex is the most difficult one to come to terms with – who indeed has collected anthropological accounts of it since Bourke's *Scatalogical Rites of All Nations*, published in 1891? – but Erikson really should have known better. All this was mere bowdlerizing of Freudian doctrine, and the whole aim of the procedure was suspect, based as it was on the doctrine of cultural relativity. 'This impression of complete diversity of nations', Róheim went on, 'is largely created by the Oedipus complex, that is to say, the Oedipus complex of the anthropologist or psychiatrist or psychologist. He does not know his own Oedipus complex – he therefore *scotomizes* clear evidence for the Oedipus complex, even when his training ought to enable him to see it.'[36] (To scotomize is what Nelson did when putting his telescope to

[32] Róheim, p.3.
[33] Devereux, p.367.
[34] Róheim, pp.369f.
[35] Róheim, p.304.
[36] Róheim, p.363.

his blind eye.)

This is a problem that anthropologists and later analysts have followed up in their own way. The Culture and Personality school must have felt vexed when one of their members compared their various psychological assessments of the Pueblo people and found them pointing in different directions – and similarly with the Ojibwa. Was this the result of sampling errors or of ethnocentric, perhaps of egocentric bias? Or, now we know what Margaret Mead was doing in Samoa, of a large proseletyzing ambition?[37]

These questions seem not to have bothered British anthropology. Evans-Pritchard, of course, had been converted to another faith, and so had laid his bets elsewhere; and if some, like Eva Meyerowitz, tended back to Frazer, or rather to Robert Graves, others like Layard took up with Jung. But the task of 'tracing the pattern of instinctive and emotional life in the texture of the social fabric', as Malinowski had put it, was too well geared to functionalism not to proceed on orthodox lines. The attitude is wonderfully exemplified by Meyer Fortes feeling the life of the Tallensi along the threads of the web of kinship, and seeing in their rites – that is, in those set moments when individuals are made persons in the light of social necessity – the constant moral of *pietas*.[38] And in this he did better than the infidel Freud, who ended his life pessimistic about the therapeutic value of psychoanalysis in the long run, but had nothing more to offer.

It was otherwise in the United States, and the reason was – to make a *bon mot* of it – if the British then still had an Empire, the Americans were always having immigrants. Hence, of course, the enquiry into national character and cultural relativism. But it now appeared that if cultures were relative to persons, and to other cultures relative to each other, the only universal around was a tautology.

Culture and Personality studies thus went back to the Oedipus complex for a saving absolute. The credit for this is due to John – and Beatrice – Whiting, who put Freud into the Human Relations Area Files as objectively as they knew how. First there was a concerted

[37] Victor Barnouw, 'Wisconsin Ojibwa culture and personality', in Spindler. Cf. Derek Freeman, *Margaret Mead and Samoa* (Harvard, 1983).

[38] Meyer Fortes, 'Pietas in ancestor worship', *Journal of the Royal Anthropological Society*, 9 (1961); and *Oedipus and Job in West African Religion* (Cambridge, 1959).

effort to redefine Freud's basic concepts in such a way that they could be subjected to empirical test, by integrating them with the concepts and principles of both learning and behaviour theory and those of cultural anthropology.[39] Soon Whiting was ready to explain circumcision, or rather to demonstrate 'a set of positive cross-cultural correlations among post-partum sex taboos, exclusive mother-son sleeping arrangements, genital mutilation, polygyny, patrilocality, patrilineality, and a tropical environment'.[40] The argument that puts these matters into a logically causal chain is not to be missed, though too long to deliver now; an elegant Rube Goldberg contraption, La Barre called it with some reason. What was wrong here was not only the locus of meaning, he went on, but the 'unexamined semantic predicament. For who cares about seventy per cent truths anyway?' As for the real locus: in his view, 'the Semites have already explained the real motive for circumcision in their abundant documents, though it depends on only a single constantly reiterated and deeply imbricated symbol, the immortal snake'.[41]

True, the immortal snake may be held responsible for a great number of things: it is not called the Tempter for nothing, and can fittingly be seen as the totem of psychoanalysis. But to make it responsible for everything puts one into another kind of predicament. For why, in that case, does the immortal snake get itself circumcised in some parts of the world and not in others? It was to this problem that Whiting addressed himself, and he at least posited certain social regularities on which the symbol could reiterate itself until its surplusage had to be cut off. He was to admit the frailty of this particular hypothesis, but his general method has been sharpened up to produce some notable results. Indeed, one such development has brought the crows home to roost on Freud himself, not to mention La Barre. This is the Bargaining Theory set out by K.E. and J.M. Paige[42] which is put to work on the incidence of cicumcision rites by means of Meyer Fortes's moralizing insight into what he called the

[39] John and Beatrice Whiting, 'A strategy for psychocultural research', in Spindler, p.43.

[40] K.E. and J.M. Paige, *The Politics of Reproductive Ritual* (Berkeley and Los Angeles, 1981), p.10.

[41] Weston La Barre, 'The clinic and the field', in Spindler, p.274.

[42] K.E. and J.M. Paige, chapter 4.

Dilemma of Fission. As they say, this is not very different from the dilemma of the Oedipus complex. First there is the expansion of the family, marked by the birth of the first child, the family's social and political resources expanding as more children are born. The marriage of the first child, however, marks the beginning of contraction for the family, for the new fathers now have jural authority over themselves and their own progeny. But under certain conditions, members of the elder generation can maintain their power in what is called a segmentary lineage system. This is marked by strong fraternal interest groups to counter the equally strong authority of the lineage head, chronic internal war and feuds, a tight contractual control over women and marriage, and circumcision. But far from circumcision being used to impress any particular cultural norm on the child – how could it, if practised on an infant? – it is the bargaining counter the lineage head uses to wield his authority over the boy's father in exchange for the protection that other members of his fellowship can give him. We can thus understand why it is that the father so often does his best to protect his son, and is not himself the circumciser; on the contrary, the circumciser can be seen as the representative of the group whose alliance is being sought – for instance, in Australia, he can be the boy's future father-in-law.

I have greatly compressed the argument, which is both neat and commodious; and I refer to it here, not because it is true, but because it may be. Consider, for a start, the fact that amongst those who make up the case-book for this hypothesis are the Semites, and let us argue backwards. We have found Freud to be the heir of Jewish mystical thought, and to have had some very ambivalent reactions to Moses; so can we not also see in the segmentary lineage system the conditions that regulate his character and ideation? For it seems that the story of the Primal Horde is altogether in the spirit of the Paige hypothesis: the tyranny of the fathers in both cases produces a strong fraternal interest group which can only act together because of the tyranny exercised over them. And we can perhaps understand now why Freud started the story with a catastrophe, bequeathed to subsequent generations through the inheritance of acquired characteristics: this was to account for the birth of the idea of fatherhood. In the Paige hypothesis we see that this depends on the fact that there is a grandfather about, that is a lineage head: and it is in this temporal sequence that the distinction between a biological and a social father can be created. On Freud's hypothesis, however, the father-figure contains the idea of the grandfather, and the sequence is compressed into one generation; and though he had it shoot out like a jack-in-the-box when the primal murder opened the lid, he was so uneasy about the grandfather's theological status that he installed it in the memory as an acquired characteristic.

All this can only strengthen one's suspicions that Freud was as haunted by the guilt of patriarchal consciousness as David Bakan has made out. The conflation of father and grandfather is certainly one of the stumbling blocks he put in the way of anthropology, and despite R.D. Laing's counter-demonstration,[43] it continues to bedevil psychoanalytic and psychiatric practice. But equally to the point we are now in danger of entering the kind of circular argument Culture and Personality studies got into: it seems that we can explain the explainer in terms of the conditions that give rise to his explanation. In any case, if Freud, in *Totem and Taboo*, allows us to say that 'hysteria is a caricature of a work of art, that an obsessional neurosis is a caricature of a religion and that a paranoiac delusion is a caricature of a philosophical system',[44] we can now ask what psychoanalysis is a caricature of. The answer, I think, must be of a philosophical system – of an ego philosophy whose psychology is always at war with the autology it proposes. In psychoanalysis, this war goes under the name of transference and counter-transference reactions, and it entails the question of observer-bias the Culture and Personality school had to face. But, as Devereux has insisted, this is at the heart of any human science: the watchword must be Know Thyself, and enquiry – whether by anthropologists or psychoanalysts – must learn to use the problems which this sets up and not ignore them.[45]

Devereux has further developed these autological problems by an appeal to Bohr's *Abtötungsprinzip*, which says that 'an overly precise study or even explanation destroys that which is observed'. Thus, he says,

[43] *The Politics of the Family* (London, 1971).
[44] *SE*, 17.13.
[45] Devereux, p.402.

> excessive sociological explanation causes the disappearance of the very object of sociological discourse, leaving in its place only what is most psychological about man. The reverse is also true, of course. Such overdone explanatory discourses within *one* frame of reference also become automatically tautological. Of course, were it possible to enunciate simultaneously two complementary discourses (which is impossible) the result would be a vicious circle. Hence, complementarity is not a 'theory' but a methodological generalization only.[46]

May I now retrace my steps. We started with an anthropological view of totemism, that is, of a collective ritual organization, and found it in danger of being enslaved by its psychoanalytic interpretation, that is, the totemic organization within the psyche. The interpretation, however, has paranoid features, created by the collectivity that gave it birth: yet it denies this collectivity more than a passing share in the creation of the Oedipal person, except at the mythological moment of its birth. In this scheme the Oedipal person becomes mantled with an absolute, the idea of fatherhood, and the culture it produces is merely an historical, that is, a relative affair. But anthropologists, whether or not they be ethologically minded, see things from the other side: persons are the results of individual bargaining within a collective, to which honour must first be given.

Róheim acknowledged this counter-claim in his remark that 'the essence of human nature is not merely that *it is conditioned* but also that *it conditions*',[47] but without relinquishing the claim of psychoanalysis to be treated as the unifying factor in the equation, and thus to be responsible for the ultimate construction of a general autology.

But what kind of autology can this be, that creates two complementary disciplines that negate each other? The spectators of this argument will do well to remember Bateson amongst the Iatmul. 'The problems which most exercise the Iatmul mind,' he wrote,

> appear to us as fundamentally unreal. There is, for example, a standing argument between the Sun moiety and the Mother moiety as

[46] Devereux, p.382.
[47] Róheim, p.435.

> to the nature of Night. While the Sun people claim Day as their totemic property, the Mother people claim Night and have developed an elaborate esoteric rigmarole about mountains meeting in the sky, and ducks, and the Milky Way to explain its existence. The Sun people are contemptuous of this and Night has become a bone of contention. The Mother people maintain that Night is a positive phenomenon due to the overlapping mountains, etc., while the Sun people maintain that Night is a mere nullity, a negation of Day, due to the absence of *their* totem, the Sun.[48]

Standing arguments of this kind – including the one that is the subject of this lecture – are characteristic of autological thinking in which complementary opposites each claim to be the cause of the other. Freud knew better than this in his story of the Primal Horde, where he had the two coming out of the one catastrophe; and so does Lévi-Strauss, though with no such dramatic staging. 'The prohibition of incest,' he writes,

> is in origin neither purely cultural nor purely natural, nor is it a composite mixture of elements from both nature and culture. It is the fundamental step because of which, thanks to which, but above all in which, the transition from nature to culture is accomplished. In one sense, it belongs to nature, for it is a general condition of culture. Consequently, we should not be surprised that its formal characteristic, universality, has been taken from nature. However, in another sense, it is already culture, exercising and imposing its rule on phenomena which initially are not subject to it.[49]

And so on, in the magisterial style we expect from the doubly reflective progress of two thoughts acting upon each other.

There are several interesting points which might be taken up from Lévi-Strauss's discussion of the incest taboo: for instance he denies Freud's right to explain the taboo by either psychological or historical arguments – in effect, to give a genetic account of it. The whole affair is better described in synchronic terms, which escape the paradoxes of self-reference by using a semantic algebra, whose formal characteristics can be demonstrated in that diagram he calls

[48] Gregory Bateson, *Naven* (London, 1980), p.229.

[49] *The Elementary Structures of Kinship*, revised edition and translation ed. Rodney Needham (Boston, 1969), p.24.

the Totemic Operator.[50] In this he sets out a system of correspondences through which the individuals of a society can recognize clan affiliations by putting parts of the body into structural opposition with natural species. This, then, is the autology of the situation; and if it has a psychology, it disappears in the grammatical rules that formulate its workings, just as its history disappears into its structure.

And, of course, the Oedipus complex disappears as well. In structuralism, the whole burden of the incest taboo is placed on the relationship of brother and sister, not of mother and son; we are once more back with Malinowski's findings in the Trobriands, and Kardiner's remarks on the mild Electra complex he suspected amongst the Marquesans. Structuralism – like anthropology in general – thus avoids the infantile situation altogether, concentrating instead on how adults operate the incest taboo when exchanging women. But there are unsuspected snags to be found in these simplicities for, as Devereux has remarked, 'the exchange of women is governed not by equity but by the rule of talion ... Primitive exchanges of women, like modern swinging, serve to ward off anxiety over homosexual retaliation for heterosexual seduction. What matters in the circulation of women is, thus, not heterosexual reciprocity but the warding off of homosexual aggression'.[51]

Structuralism and psychoanalysis can thus censure each other for a number of faults. Yet they are in complete agreement about the essential point: that the incest taboo is the complementary aspect of the birth of Rule. All things, we may then say, start with Rule, especially Freudian psychology: for this cannot be said to exist before the incest taboo created the complementary twins Nature and Culture. Rule creates psychoanalysable moments, but cannot itself by psychoanalysed, nor should psychoanalysis presume to occupy the throne of rule: Frazer has already described where this leads to, namely the sacrifice of the sacred king. Nor can it do more than colour the classificatory activity of the mind, which from the start is that of Rule itself.

Ricoeur has characterized this position as being Kantism without a transcendental subject; he sees in its workings 'a Kantian rather

[50] Lévi-Strauss, *The Savage Mind* (London, 1966), p.152.
[51] Devereux, p.387.

than a Freudian unconscious, a combinative, categorizing unconscious ...'; also a 'categorizing system unconnected with a thinking subject ... homologous with nature; it may perhaps be nature',[52] and Lévi-Strauss has acknowledged the finesse and perspicacity of these observations. Structuralism is thus a new kind of autology: it dispenses with the usual traits thought to signify the psychic unity of mankind, by subsuming them in a more general and far-reaching imperative. All the same, it cannot escape from the paradox all autologies must contain, and if it may be identified as a form of Sun totem, though operating on a meta-level, we must expect to find a co-nascent Mother totem as its complement. We need, that is, to restore the conflict element, which Lévi-Strauss has semantically exorcized, to its place in real time, with the thinking and feeling subject as the representative of social order: that is, the universals of structuralism should be complemented by the universals of interactive process.

Is a marriage between anthropology and psychoanalysis then possible, despite the logical inconsistence of their relationship? We are once more caught in the double bind, and if there is an escape from it the originator of the concept should have some useful advice. This, of course, is Gregory Bateson, whose study of Naven led him inescapably to the idea once he had formulated social life in terms of a self-regulatory system based on cybernetic process, and had unfolded the problems of self-reference into the logic of meta-language so as to distinguish the nature of an explanation from the matters it takes up. Add to this a theory of higher-order learning, and the conflict element will be seen to operate certain sequential relations that are as much psychological as sociological. The cybernetic explanation stops these complementarities from nullifying each other's existence, by making both depend on a common timing: Time, in fact, can now be acknowledged as an aspect of Order itself.

All this is still a long way from being realized in practice, and Kant may still prove indigestible to General Systems Theory. Meanwhile anthropology and psychoanalysis continue to provoke each other into fresh activity whenever they are made aware of each other. The battlefield was long ago demarcated by Theodor Reik: 'two factors determine the fate of the individual and that of races,' he

[52] Lévi-Strauss, *The Raw and the Cooked* (London, 1970), p.11.

wrote: 'disposition and experience, *daimon* and *tyche.*'[53] From the beginning psychoanalysis claimed the *daimon* as its own, isolating it within the individual psyche and letting anthropology make what it could of mere experience; anthropology countering such moves by installing the *daimon* in the collectivity, to whose categories it assigns some kind of independent and not fortuitous existence. The argument, if formally proper, may still be fundamentally unreal: but I must end this lecture by observing the proprieties, and paying respect to the Sun Totem and the Mother Totem, whose disputations I have here attempted to describe.

[53] Reik, p.20.

CHAPTER SEVEN

Psychoanalysis and the Study of the Ancient World

Hugh Lloyd-Jones

The term psychoanalysis, strictly speaking, should denote only the method of Freud and his followers. But I shall say a little about the analytic psychology of Jung and the symbolic theory of Ernst Cassirer; and since structuralists ground their interpretation of myth on the assumption that its structure reflects that of the human psyche, I shall speak briefly of the structuralist approach to myth.

We need to guard against attributing to the influence of psychoanalysis many features of the intellectual climate of our time that may well derive at least in part, directly or indirectly, from other sources. Thomas Mann, in the oration which he delivered in Vienna on Freud's eightieth birthday in 1936,[1] congratulated Freud on having achieved all that he had achieved without knowing Nietzsche, without knowing Novalis, without knowing Kierkegaard and, most remarkable of all, without knowing Schopenhauer. The mention of Novalis was a reminder that Freudianism was rooted in Romanticism, a fact strongly borne out by Dr Storr's lecture; both Kierkegaard and Nietzsche anticipated many notions which the popular imagination would ascribe to Freud; and the id and the ego bear an obvious resemblance to the Will and Idea in Schopenhauer's philosophy. Much of the influence of psychoanalysis upon classical studies has been exerted indirectly, above all through anthropology.

If one were to arrange the matter chronologically, it would fall

[1] English version in *Essays of Three Decades* (London, 1947).

under the headings supplied by three periods. First came the pioneer days up till the end of the first war, when Freud and his disciples made occasional forays into the study of myth; then the period between the wars, when psychoanalysts, and still more other psychologists, kept up some activity in this domain, while classical scholars for the most part remained aloof; and finally the post-war period. Early in this, one classical scholar seemed to have fulfilled Freud's prediction that the successful application of psychoanalysis to the ancient world was likelier to be made by classical scholars with some knowledge of psychology than by psychologists with some knowledge of antiquity; he published an important book which bore obvious marks of psychoanalytic influence, falling for the most part within the realm of social psychology. After that classical scholars, especially in America, overcame their previous hesitation. Many assumed that psychoanalysis would provide them with a golden key, and hastened to apply it to all locks, without stopping to ask themselves what doors it might reasonably be expected to open or what they might expect to find behind them. But it will be best to arrange the material not chronologically, but according to the subject-matter.

Firstly, then, I shall speak of attempts to psychoanalyse characters in history; secondly, of attempts to psychoanalyse characters in literature, or authors; thirdly, of studies of ancient psychology and of verbal therapy that have made use of psychoanalysis; fourthly, of the use made of psychoanalysis in the interpretation of myth; and lastly of the application to the study of antiquity of a social psychology influenced by psychoanalysis.

The chill of the cold winds that are now blowing upon psychoanalysis from many quarters[2] is nowhere felt more keenly than in the domain of psychohistory. Attempts to produce psychological case-histories of historical characters have convinced few historians; nor have those devoted to persons who lived recently enough for a large quantity of data to be available, like Woodrow Wilson or Gandhi, fared much better than those aimed at persons long dead, like Leonardo da Vinci or Martin Luther. In the case of

[2] On psychohistory in particular see Jacques Barzun, *Clio and the Doctors* (Chicago and London, 1974); David E. Stannard, *Shrinking History: On Freud and the Failure of Psychohistory* (New York and Oxford, 1980).

ancient history, the prospects of successful psychoanalysis are obviously limited by the paucity of information; and they are still further restricted by the unwillingness of ancient writers to furnish the kind of information which might make such a study possible.

It happens that the possibility of such analysis was investigated, from the start of his career, by one of the most intelligent ancient historians living, Hermann Strasburger.[3] His grandfather had helped to advance Freud in his academic career, and he himself read Freud with enthusiasm as a student in the early 1930s. His friendship with the neurologist Arthur Muthmann and the psychologist Karl Kleist encouraged him in the attempt to apply Freudian methods in the study of ancient personalities; but this hope was doomed to disappointment. Strasburger found that the kind of information transmitted to us by ancient biographers and historians, even in the case of such celebrated persons as Alexander the Great and Julius Caesar, is not of the intimate personal kind which would be necessary for an effective analysis; and that those who had speculated about their psychological make-up had been reduced to making inferences that lacked any secure base. Often such inferences have been invalidated by the psychohistorian's ignorance of ancient cultures; for instance the report that both men indulged in homosexual activity cannot be construed as it might in the case of modern persons, for the prevailing attitude to homosexuality was different, and it was common for the same person to behave at different times in a homosexual and in a heterosexual way. We know that Alexander drank heavily, and his early death has been ascribed by some to alcoholism; but Strasburger points out that the social habits of the Macedonian court made it inevitable that the king should consume large quantities of drink, and we cannot be sure that Alexander drank more than other important Macedonians. Strasburger is responsible for some of the most important modern work on Julius Caesar, about whom we have far more information recorded by contemporaries or near-contemporaries than we have about Alexander. But the one important conclusion he has been able to reach about a matter that might affect Caesar's psychology is that the assertion of certain ancient writers that he was an epileptic must

[3] See 'Psychoanalyse und alte Geschichte', *Studien zur Alten Geschichte* (Hildesheim, 1982), 2.1098f.

be false; doctors have assured Strasburger that no epileptic could have been capable of the sustained physical and mental activity displayed by Caesar.

We possess three collections of letters by ancient authors to which the would-be analyst might expect that he might turn, those of Cicero, Seneca[4] and Pliny. A moment's reflection will show that the highly stylized compositions of the two latter could not be expected to throw light on the psychology of their authors. At first sight Cicero seems a more promising case; we have many letters of his addressed to an intimate friend whose complete sympathy and known discretion made it easy for Cicero, a man who found it as easy to pour out what was in his mind as James Boswell or Queen Victoria, to confide to him his every thought. However, Cicero's confessions are not of the kind that lend themselves to psychological interpretation, unless the analyst is willing to risk speculation that is insecurely based. Though Cicero was twice married and divorced, though he loved his children dearly and was plunged into the darkest depression by his daughter's death, we find nothing in his correspondence that illuminates his most intimate personal feelings in the way an analyst might find helpful.

The period of Roman decline, which E.R. Dodds, borrowing a phrase from Auden, termed an 'age of anxiety', might seem likely to provide better material for psychohistory. Dodds himself has paid attention to the successful rhetorician Aelius Aristides, who lived during the second century after Christ.[5] This person seemed on the threshold of a great career when he was prostrated by a complex of maladies recalling those which affected Proust; he appears to have suffered from asthma and from various forms of hypertension, producing headaches, insomnia and severe gastric troubles. He derived comfort from his special relationship with the divine healer Ascelpius, whose cult had been important since the late fifth century before Christ. He records innumerable dreams, which have been classified under three main types. Some, in which he enjoys sensational triumphs, harmonize with Freud's theory of dreams as

[4] See, however, the psychoanalysis of Seneca by E. Phillips Barker in the *Oxford Classical Dictionary*, 1st edition (1949).

[5] *The Greeks and the Irrational* (Berkeley and Los Angeles, 1951), pp.109f., 113f.; *Pagan and Christian in an Age of Anxiety* (Cambridge, 1965), pp.39f.

wish-fulfilments; but others belong to the category of those anxiety dreams which form such an awkward exception to Freud's theory, and others, in which the patron god appeared to him and advised him, to that category of revelatory dreams which is indeed commonest in the ancient world but which is not unknown in the medieval and Renaissance periods. These three types of dream, together with symbolic dreams and daytime visions, make up the five categories under which dreams are classified by Artemidorus of Daldis, a contemporary of Aristides and the author of the only one of many books on dream interpretation to have survived from antiquity entire. It is not often easy to invest one of Aristides's dreams with sexual meaning, and they are a good deal better suited by Dr Rycroft's theory of the dream as a message from one portion of the self to another[6] than they are by that of Freud. The same is true, as Dr Rycroft has observed, of most of the dreams recorded and classified by Artemidorus and by the early fifth-century Latin writer Macrobius.

The ancient author who at first sight seems to provide most material for a psychoanalytic study is St Augustine, whose early family circumstances seem so strangely like those of D.H. Lawrence. He tells us that his mother St Monica wished God to become father of her son in place of the unsatisfactory Patricius, causing Peter Brown to observe that 'by remarks like these, Augustine has deservedly brought down upon his own head the attention of modern psychological interpreters'.[7] Among these have been no lesser persons than Rebecca West and Dodds, who in 1927-8 published an article called 'St Augustine's *Confessions*: a study in spiritual maladjustment'.[8] 'It is, however, one thing,' Brown writes,

> to take due note of a blatant childhood tension that was still very much alive in Augustine's mind as he wrote the *Confessions* in middle age, and it is quite another to follow this tension through, from its roots in Augustine's childhood, throughout a long and varied life. The unexpected combinations, ramifications and resolutions that a proper knowledge of modern psychology would lead us to expect escape the historian.

[6] *The Innocence of Dreams* (London, 1979).

[7] *Augustine of Hippo: A Biography* (London, 1967), p.31 with n.4.

[8] Rebecca West, *St Augustine* (London, 1933); Dodds, *Hibbert Journal*, 26 (1927-8).

These and other attempts of the kind, Brown writes, show that it is as difficult as it is desirable to combine competence as a historian with sensitivity as a psychologist.

Even less successful than psychohistory has been the attempt to psychoanalyse ancient imaginative writers or characters from their work. The American scholar R.S. Caldwell has found in all of Aeschylus's plays an Oedipal pattern; the effect of a father upon his children is, in his view, 'the most important single element in the work of Aeschylus'.[9] Xerxes comes to grief through an attempt to outdo Darius; Eteocles and Polynices because of an incestuous rivalry with Oedipus. The daughters of Danaus 'typify the oedipal situation' (though it was their husbands that they killed). Although Prometheus is not the son of Zeus, he contrives to have an Oedipal relation to him; Aegisthus is 'the paradigm of the son's oedipal fancy, the essential basis of all heroic myth, to return from exile, kill the father and marry the mother'.[10] Writers of the same kind have a good deal to say about Orestes, with whom Mr Caldwell seems to have confused Aegisthus.

Plato may seem to offer a more promising subject for analysis than any of the poets, and the American analyst Bennett Simon has tried to analyse him.[11] After his father's death, Plato's mother married a widower with a son, and they had another son; Plato, Simon thinks, did not know and label the Oedipal conflicts that resulted, but his dialogues contain 'repeated references' to parricidal and incestuous wishes. Plato, he says, 'struggled with oedipal impulses, and may have felt a certain Hamlet-like outrage at his mother's remarriage and subsequent child-bearing'; he 'struggled to master some primal scene, or at least was very much caught up with a primal scene fantasy'. This seems not much more helpful than Caldwell's effort and it seems clear enough that anyone who wishes to psychoanalyse an ancient author is likely to find himself fatally handicapped by the paucity of the data and their reluctance to lend themselves to

[9] 'The pattern of Aeschylean tragedy', *Transactions of the American Philological Association*, 101 (1970); the same author has discussed the *Seven Against Thebes* in *Arethusa*, 6 (1973), and the *Suppliants* in *Arethusa*, 7 (1974).

[10] Cf. R.S. Caldwell, 'Selected bibliography on psychoanalysis and the classics', *Arethusa*, 7 (1974), pp.121f. and 125f.; Justin Glenn, 'Psychoanalytic writings on classical mythology and religion', *Classical World*, 70 (1976-7), pp.235f.

[11] Bennett Simon, *Mind and Madness in Ancient Greece: The Classical Roots of Modern Psychiatry* (Ithaca, 1978), p.210.

analytic purposes.

George Devereux has pronounced that 'the critical explanation of great literature may perhaps be too important a matter to be entrusted to philologists',[12] and over the last thirty years he has done his best to rescue classical literature from such a fate. He is a learned and gifted scholar, with a wide knowledge of psychology and anthropology, besides clinical experience in psychiatry and field experience in the study of remote tribes. But his applications of psychoanalysis to literature – I do not speak of myth – has for the most part been vitiated by his obstinate refusal to bear in mind the vital differences that separate a work of conscious art from data collected in the course of psychiatric practice. His book on the interpretation of dreams in Greek tragedy contains, like all his writings, isolated observations of great interest; but as an interpretation of literature it has rightly been judged a total failure,[13] because of his stubborn refusal to remember that a dream described in a drama is an invention of the dramatist, who puts into it what is required by his artistic purpose. Just so, Devereux read the famous poem in which Sappho describes the symptoms of passion as though it was a record of clinical experience, such as the anxiety attacks which he claimed to have witnessed in homosexual patients, provoked by envy of a rival; it was left to the despised philologists to explain Sappho's words in terms of her poetic purpose and to relate them to the tradition within which she worked.[14]

On occasion a writer acquainted with psychoanalysis has made mildly interesting comments on some episode in a work of literary art, as when Devereux pointed out that the method by which in the *Bacchae* of Euripides Cadmus recalls his daughter Agaue from the God-induced frenzy in which she has helped to kill her son resembles a technique used by psychiatrists today.[15] Even before psychoanalysis became widely known, it had been realized that the madness of Ajax and Heracles in the tragedies called after them is described

[12] *Psychoanalytic Quarterly*, 26 (1957), p.385.

[13] *Dreams in Greek Tragedy* (Oxford, 1976); see Bernard Knox, *TLS*, 10 December 1976, p.1534, and M.R. Lefkowitz, *Heroines and Hysterics* (London, 1981), pp.77f.

[14] Devereux, 'The nature of Sappho's seizure in fr.31 L.-P. as evidence of her inversion', *Classical Quarterly*, 20 (1970); against, see Lefkowitz, *Heroines and Hysterics*, pp.59f.

[15] *Journal of Hellenic Studies*, 90 (1970).

in realistic detail. But psychoanalysis has contributed little, if anything, to the critical understanding of Greek literature; the purpose of the authors is too different from that of the analyst to provide him with the kind of data he would need. With a few exceptions, not including the apparent one of Shakespeare, this seems to be true of all literature before that Romantic period in which the roots of Freudianism lie. Let me take as a specimen an attempted analysis which because it is superior to most of its kind is well calculated to reveal that kinds' essential limitations.

In 1974 Anne V. Rankin published an article called 'Euripides' *Hippolytus*; a psychopathological hero'.[16] Taking her inspiration from Freud's brief article on psychopathological characters in literature, Mrs Rankin remarked reasonably enough that Hippolytus's aversion to women must be connected with his birth as the son of the man-hunting Amazon carried off by Theseus, and from here goes on to speculate about his psychological make-up rather as if he were a person in a trial she had just read about in the newspaper. He must have first directed at his foster-nurse 'the infantile neurotic cathexis which he scarcely had time to develop in relation to his mother; later, 'by taking Artemis as a mother-surrogate, Hippolytus can give expression in his worship to his longing for his mother figure without any concomitant feeling of shame at his illegitimacy'. He goes hunting because of his unconscious libidinal cathexis attached to Artemis; the woods symbolize pubic hair, the meadows where he picks flowers to offer them to the goddess symbolize the female genitals. Speculation about the human type to which the Euripidean Hippolytus, had he been a real person, might have belonged may evidently be of interest to a certain type of reader, just as when served up, as in this instance, without the faintest grain of humour, it may offer entertainment to another. But Mrs Rankin is no more throwing light upon the art of Euripides than Mrs Cowden-Clarke was throwing light upon the art of Shakespeare when she wrote her Victorian best-seller *The Girlhood of Shakespeare's Heroines*. Those who heard the highly entertaining lectures which Professor Bernard Knox gave in Oxford some years ago will remember that he offered some almost unbelievable examples of this kind of method from American books and journals. Since the last war, to acquire a

[16] *Arethusa*, 7 (1974).

smattering of Freud, usually untainted by the smallest admixture of more modern psychology, has been one way of solving the perennial problem of how to publish work on Greek literature and not perish, without knowing any Greek.

The history of ancient psychology has naturally been studied from the standpoint of psychoanalysis; so has the ancient treatment of mental illness and other complaints which may be treated by auto-suggestion or by verbal therapy. A comprehensive treatment of both topics has been attempted by Bennett Simon, a psychiatrist who knows Greek, and he has collected some valuable material, though handicapped by the strain of naivety evinced by the analysis of Plato which I have already mentioned. In a general way scholars are now more sympathetic than their nineteenth-century predecessors to the treatment of disease in early Greece by such magical and religious methods as ceremonies of purification, the chanting of spells designed to expel supernatural beings from possessed persons, and incubation in temples in the hope of a cure. 'No straightforward account,' Geoffrey Lloyd writes in his fine book *Magic, Reason and Experience*,[17] 'in which "science" and "philosophy" together in unison stand opposed to "magic" and "the irrational", can be sustained in face of the evident complexities both *within* and *between* the theory and practice of medicine on the one hand and that of the investigation of nature on the other.' But the influence of psychoanalysis is by no means the only fact that is responsible for this change; and as the quotations in this part of Lloyd's book indicate, it has been exerted for the most part indirectly, through the anthropologists.

The pioneer of psychology in ancient times was Plato, whom Werner Jaeger in 1943 called the father of psychoanalysis,[18] and whose relation to his alleged progeny has naturally been explored. As early as 1915 Nachmanson compared Plato's Eros with Freud's libido, a comparison worked out in detail by Thomas Gould in his book *Platonic Love*, where, as a reviewer said, the writer's preoccupation with Freud tends to obscure rather than illuminate his thesis.[19] Simon devotes to Plato three chapters which are not the

[17] Cambridge, 1979, p.49.

[18] *Paideia*, 2 (1943), p.340.

[19] M. Nachmanson, *Internationale Zeitschrift für Psychoanalyse*, 3 (1915); see Glenn, 'Psychoanalytic writings on Greek and Latin authors', *Classical World*, 66 (1972), pp.184f.; Caldwell, 'Selected bibliography', pp.128f.; Gould, *Platonic Love* (London, 1963).

most rewarding portion of his book. The best modern studies of Platonic psychology known to me are two by Dodds,[20] who showed how Plato 'side by side with the intellectualist theory which he had inherited from Socrates and the Sophists comes to recognize an irrational factor within the mind itself, and so gradually develops a deeper view of moral evil as being the result of psychological conflict'. Dodds thought highly of the psychological insight of Aristotle, who, in his view, together with his pupils 'appreciated better perhaps than any Greeks the necessity of studying the irrational factors in behaviour if we are to reach a realistic understanding of human nature'. He would have liked to devote a whole chapter to Aristotle's treatment of the subject, and it is a pity that he never did so, especially since this part of Aristotle's work is now receiving much attention from philosophers. Dodds is critical of the Hellenistic philosophers, who in his view went back behind Plato and Aristotle to the naive intellectualism of their predecessors. No doubt Dodds's interest in psychoanalysis sharpened his interest in the psychology of the philosophers, but it is hard to see that it influenced his actual treatment. He voiced the suspicion that 'had Plato lived today, he would have been profoundly interested in the new depth psychology, but appalled by the tendency to reduce human reason to an instrument for rationalizing unconscious impulses'.[21] That was surely Dodds's own attitude, and Freud, who always called himself a rationalist, would have concurred in it, at least in theory.

No department of the study of the ancient world has been more affected by psychoanalysis than the study of myth. In this region the classical scholar has the great advantage of having a learned, sober and judicious guide in G.S. Kirk, whose two books, *Myth: Its Meaning and Functions* and *The Nature of Greek Myths*, are indispensable. 'There have been three major developments in the

[20] *The Ancient Concept of Progress* (Oxford, 1974), pp.106f. and chapter 7 of *The Greeks and the Irrational.*

[21] *The Greeks and the Irrational*, p.218. Cf. Erich Fromm, *Sigmund Freud's Mission* (London, 1959), p.115: 'while Freud represented the culmination of rationalism, he struck at the same time a fatal blow against rationalism ... he undermined the rationalistic picture that man's intellect dominated the scene without restriction or challenge. In this respect, the vision of the power of the forces of the underworld, Freud was an heir of Romanticism, the movement which tried to penetrate the sphere of the non-rational'. Professor Mary Lefkowitz, after listening to Dr Storr's lecture in this series, remarked to me, 'Freud tried to make Romanticism into a science'.

modern study of myth,' he writes. 'The first was the realization, associated with Tylor, Frazer and Durkheim, that the myths of primitive societies are highly relevant to the subject as a whole. The second was Freud's discovery of the unconscious and its relation to myths and dreams. The third is the structural theory of myth propounded by Claude Lévi-Strauss.'[22]

In his book on the interpretation of dreams, Freud argued that myths and dreams often work in the same way, and that the mind functions in both by means of the so-called primary processes of condensation, displacement and symbolization, disregarding the categories of space and time and relieving tension by means of wish-fulfilling illusions. Freud is the inventor of the notion, later even more strongly insisted on by Karl Abraham[23] and later still by Jung,[24] that myths are a product of the collective unconscious, and can be regarded as 'the dream-thinking of the people'. This takes one straight back to Herder and the beginnings of Romanticism; Durkheim, by his talk of 'collective representations', tried to make use of the concept while avoiding responsibility for its obvious metaphysical element. Kirk[25] points out what to me seems the obvious fact that there can be no such thing as the collective unconscious; myths, like dreams, must be the products of individual minds. Yet Kirk allows that 'the manipulation of emotions and experiences, at a less than fully conscious level, does seem to be implied in those myths that bear on social and personal preoccupations'. True, many myths seem to have a dream-like quality; many myths reveal a symbolism like that found in dreams, and it seems likely that a myth, like a work of literary art, may have implications of which its author was not fully conscious. But that is because something very like the primary processes is required for the composition of any imaginative writing; and since that composition is intentional, it must be distinguished from the process of dreaming, which, however coherent and meaningful some dreams may be, is not directed by the conscious mind. Freud's assumption that the activity is essentially irrational and indeed neurotic seems to me

[22] Kirk, *Myth: Its Meaning and Functions in Ancient and Other Cultures* (Cambridge, 1970), p.429.

[23] *Dreams and Myths* (New York, 1913).

[24] See Anthony Storr, *Jung* (London, 1973), especially chapter 3.

[25] Kirk, *Myth*, chapter 6.

mistaken; as Dr Rycroft, following Susanne Langer puts it, 'symbolization is a basic human need, not a symptom produced by conflict and repression, and human behaviour is a language, not a set of mechanisms for discharging tensions'.[26] Langer's distinction between the discursive symbolism that is conveyed in language and the non-discursive symbolism of the dream seems to me highly relevant to the distinction between dream and myth, one which the effect of psychoanalysis has tended to blur in a confusing fashion. Myth is a kind of fiction, and students of myth should give more attention to the kind of considerations discussed by Bettelheim in *The Uses of Enchantment.*[27]

By rejecting the belief in the collective unconscious and insisting on the distinction between dreams and myths, I have already indicated a fundamental disagreement with the analytic philosophy of Jung.[28] In 1951 Jung collaborated with the Hungarian classical scholar Karl Kerenyi in a book called *Introduction to a Scientific Mythology*, a title which, as Kirk has pointed out, recalls the fatuous optimism of Max Müller. In many subsequent works Kerenyi tried to apply Jung's theories to classical material, though in his later work he seems to have deviated in the direction of the less abstract approach to myth of Walter F. Otto. Jung was more sympathetic to myth than Freud, as he was more sympathetic to emotion, and was more aware of the valuable function which it has performed and still performs within the complex of human society. He claimed to find in Greek society, as in every other, the same series of archetypes – the earth-mother, the divine child, the sun, God, the self, animus and anima in their special Jungian sense, such shapes as the mandala and the cross, the magic number four. But the trouble is that, as Kirk and others have pointed out, the archetypes cannot be shown to be anything like so pervasive as the theory requires that they should be. In any case, all of them are likely, in the normal course of human life, to figure frequently enough in myths and other fictions, so that Jung's belief that the nature of the human mind is such that these and no other set of symbols must constantly recur scarcely compels assent.

[26] *The Innocence of Dreams*, pp.13f.

[27] Bruno Bettelheim, *The Uses of Enchantment* (London, 1976).

[28] See also Kirk, *Myth*, pp.274-80, and *The Nature of Greek Myths* (Harmondsworth, 1974), pp.76f.

Hardly more convincing is the elaborate theory of mythical symbolism constructed by Ernst Cassirer.[29] His belief in an 'underlying structural form of the mythical fantasy and mythical thinking' depends firstly upon an application to the supposed language that is myth of neo-Kantian presuppositions about language that are not generally acceptable, and secondly upon the acceptance of the outdated theory of primitive mentality associated with the name of Lucien Lévy-Bruhl.

Perhaps the best way in which I can give a notion of the results attained by the methods of the different schools that have applied psychoanalysis to the interpretation of myth will be to describe a few selected specimens of their effect in action. No myth has engaged their interest more than that of Oedipus; a full account of the many and various interpretations of it that they have offered would be substantially longer than the sizeable book which Patrick Mullahy devoted to them in 1948.[30] I will speak briefly, then, of a small selection of interpretations of the myth of Oedipus, ending with some of the most recent structuralist theories put forward by French scholars.

Freud's own occasional explanations of individual myths are somewhat disappointing. His contention that the myth of Prometheus indicates that 'to gain control over fire man had to renounce the homosexually-tinged desire to put it out with a stream of urine'[31] is not often mentioned even by his loyal adherents, and his suggestion that the legend of Medusa's snaky locks epitomizes the fear of castration inspired in a small boy by the sight of female genitals[32] is not the only possible explanation of the story's origin. More interesting is the famous discussion of the myth of Oedipus in the fifth chapter of the famous book on the interpretation of dreams. It originated, Freud suggests, because all of us have thought in infancy of killing our fathers and having intercourse with our

[29] Cf. Kirk, *Myth*, pp.263f., and *The Nature of Greek Myths*, pp.79f.

[30] *Oedipus: Myth and Complex* (New York, 1948). See Glenn, 'Classical mythology', pp.230f. and Caldwell, 'Selected bibliography', pp.120f. Devereux has argued that the blinding of Oedipus is a symbolic castration, *Journal of Hellenic Studies*, 93 (1973); on this theory see R.G.A. Buxton, *Journal of Hellenic Studies*, 100 (1980).

[31] *SE*, 22.185f.; see Glenn, 'Classical mythology', p.236.

[32] *SE*, 18.273; cf. Glenn, 'Classical mythology', pp.228f. Freud's and Ferenczi's interpretations, which first appeared in 1922 and 1923 respectively, are criticized by Hazel Barnes, *The Meddling Gods* (Lincoln, Nebraska, 1974).

mothers; and he claims that his theory is confirmed by Jocasta's remark in *Oedipus Tyrannus* that many men have dreamed of incest with their mothers.[33] To call this dream the key to the tragedy was surely a mistake, for Freud's theory is relevant to the original significance of the myth, not to the use made of it in Sophocles's play, which, in Freud's own words, employs a form of the myth which 'was the result of an uncomprehending secondary elaboration of the material, which sought to give it theological intention'. How seriously one takes Freud's suggestion will depend on one's attitude to Freud's belief in the universality of the Oedipus complex, one that is not shared by most modern psychologists.

Ferenczi[34] found that Oedipus, who wished to pursue this enquiry, stood for the reality principle, whereas Jocasta, who wished him to abandon it, stood for the pleasure principle. Géza Róheim made the riddle of the Sphinx the pretext for a vast, rambling work of great learning and ingenuity and great silliness.[35] But Otto Rank, who himself denied the central importance of the Oedipus complex, threw far more light upon the myth of Oedipus. In his book *The Myth of the Birth of the Hero*[36] Rank groups that myth with a whole series of heroic myths, including those of Moses, Paris, Telephus, Cyrus, Tristan, Heracles, Christ, Siegfried and Lohengrin. In each the hero's life is endangered soon after birth; in each he is rescued by humble persons or by animals; in each he turns out to be the child of parents far greater and nobler than those who had been supposed his parents; in each he finds his real parents, often taking revenge on his real or his supposed father; finally he achieves the highest eminence. Rank presents his theory in conjunction with belief in the collective unconscious; he explains the problem posed by the recurrence of similar legends in cultures which are not likely to have influenced one another by arguing that the human psyche is so constructed that it invents similar myths at different times and places. But since human life, because of the general conditions of existence on this planet, tends at all times and places to assume patterns which in a general way are very like each other, the recurrence of such patterns

[33] *SE*, 4.261f.; *Oedipus Tyrannus*, lines 981f.

[34] S. Ferenczi, 'Symbolical representation of the pleasure and reality principles in the Oedipus myth', in *Contributions to Psycho-Analysis* (Boston, 1916).

[35] *The Riddle of the Sphinx* (London, 1934).

[36] *The Myth of the Birth of the Hero and Other Writings* (New York, 1952).

can easily be explained on an empirical basis. Their relevance to the need of the child to achieve independence from his parents can easily be seen; and if we remove the framework of psychoanalytic theory from Rank's work, we are left with a valuable contribution to comparative mythology of the kind which we now associate with the name of Vladimir Propp.[37]

Speculation about the myth of Oedipus has never ceased; space is short, and I go straight to Claude Lévi-Strauss. Treating of the myth first in 1955,[38] he dealt with it as part of the continuous history of the house of Cadmus, founder of Thebes, which he divides into eleven segments and then sets out in four columns. In column *i* he places segments which exemplify the overvaluation of kinship; that of Cadmus when he devoted his whole life to looking for his lost sister Europa, that of Oedipus when he married his mother, that of Antigone when she sacrificed her life in order to bury her brother Polynices. In column *ii* he places undervaluations of kinship; that of the giants who sprang from the dragon's teeth sewn by Cadmus when they killed each other, that of Oedipus when he killed his father, that of Eteocles and Polynices when they kill each other. In column *iii* he places the destruction of monsters by men; Cadmus kills the dragon, Oedipus kills the Sphinx. In column *iv* he places men who are themselves in some sense monsters; Labdacus is one, because his name means 'lame'; his son Laius is another, because his name means 'left'; his son Oedipus is a third, because his name means 'swellfoot'. Column *iii* signifies, I do not quite see why, denial of the autochthonous origin of man; column *iv*, because in Indian myths earth-born creatures often have strange walks, signifies the affirmation of that origin. The myth is therefore an attempt to explain how it comes about that human beings are actually born of a union between man and woman; 'although the problem cannot be solved, the myth represents a kind of logical tool,' Lévi-Strauss tells us: not a very useful tool, I feel. We must remember that his method works better for cultures which, like those of the American Indians,

[37] On V.J. Propp's *Morphology of the Folktale* (1928), see W. Burkert, *Structure and History in Greek Mythology and Ritual* (Berkeley and Los Angeles, 1979), pp.5f.

[38] 'The structural study of myth', translated in *Structural Anthropology* (Harmondsworth, 1970). Dr Ruth Padel refers me to the account of Lévi-Strauss's use of the literature influenced by Freud that is given by James A. Boon, *From Symbolism to Structuralism: Lévi-Strauss in a Literary Tradition* (Oxford, 1972).

have totemism as an important element; but it must be acknowledged that by this kind of procedure a myth like that of Oedipus could be made to yield many different patterns of about equal relevance and equal interest.

Returning many years later to the problem, in 1975, Lévi-Strauss adopted a different approach;[39] he found the theme of the riddle of the Sphinx to be that of walking. 'Not walking straight, stuttering, forgetting,' he wrote,

> are all so many converging markers which the myth uses, bound up with the themes of indiscretion and misunderstanding, in order to express the failures, distortions, or blockages of communication between different levels of social life; sexual communication, the transfer of life (normal childbirth being opposed to sterility or monstrosity), communication between successive generations (fathers transmitting their status and their function to their sons), verbal exchanges, communication of the self with the self (presence of mind, the transparency to oneself contrasting with forgetting, division, the doubling of the self, as in Oedipus).

Lévi-Strauss himself is less important with regard to Greek mythology than certain French classical scholars influenced by his methods. As long ago as 1967,[40] Jean-Pierre Vernant demolished an exaggeratedly Freudian interpretation of the Oedipus myth by Didier Anzieu, showing that it failed to take account of the myth's historical and cultural content. In 1974[41] Vernant criticized Lévi-Strauss's first attempt at interpreting it, and in 1982[42] he refined Lévi-Strauss's later suggestions so as to create an ingenious structuralist theory of his own. Vernant is influenced by the anthropology of Ignace Meyerson, which requires that the interpreter take full cognizance of the social and cultural context of the myth he would interpret, and the technical equipment which he acquired from the eminent authority on Greek law and religion

[39] 'Mythe et oubli', in *Langue, Discours, Société: pour E. Benveniste* (Paris, 1975), where he takes up again the discussion resumed at *Anthropologie structurale deux* (Paris, 1973).

[40] Translated in *Tragedy and Myth in Ancient Greece* (Brighton, 1981), pp.63f.

[41] Translated in *Myth and Society in Ancience Greece* (Brigton, 1980), pp.226f.

[42] Oddly enough, in a *Festschrift* dedicated to him by American admirers in *Arethusa*, 15 (1982).

Louis Gernet enables him to do this while making an independent and ingenious use of structuralist methods that derive from Lévi-Strauss.[43]

Taking up the latter's emphasis on walking, Vernant argues that lameness has certain advantages, producing as it does a zigzagging or oscillating gait. This makes him recall the lameness of the craftsman god Hephaestus, and also in human beings as they are depicted as severed halves of an original whole in the speech of Aristophanes in Plato's *Symposium*, and animals in the island of the sun described in the Hellenistic romance of Iambulus. One must remark that the two latter types, both belonging to imaginative fiction of a highly sophisticated kind, are scarcely relevant. But Vernant drags in also the 'lame soul' in Plato's *Republic* and the oracles that warned the Spartans to beware of the 'lame reign' of Agesilaus; the structuralist, like the magpie, builds a nest from heterogeneous materials.

Labdacus, the lame one, dies when his son is one year old. Laius, the awkward one, is driven from home and takes refuge with Pelops. Awkward in all his dealings, he 'fumbles his erotic behaviour' by seducing his host's son Chrysippus. Pelops curses him, and the oracle predicts that he will have a son who kills his father and marries his mother. Laius therefore has 'left-handed' intercourse, *a tergo*, with his wife, but one day he lapses into normal intercourse and Oedipus is born. He is exposed, but finds his way back and kills Laius. Next Vernant makes use of a little-known story by Pausanias, which makes the Sphinx a natural daughter of Laius, who tells her of an oracle given to Cadmus, the founder of the family. Laius has sons by concubines who do not know this oracle, and the Sphinx kills them for their ignorance. But Oedipus does know the oracle; the answer to the riddle is man, the only creature whose way of walking changes. But though Oedipus solves the riddle,

> instead of making him equal to the man who progresses in life by walking in a straight line, his success identifies him with the monster whom the Sphinx's words evoke: the being who is at one and the same time two-, three-, four-footed, the man who as he advances in age

[43] See his account of his own methods in relation to those of others in the article referred to in n.41 above, which is of great importance for the understanding of his work.

> jumbles up and confuses the social and cosmic order of the generations instead of respecting it. Oedipus, the two-footed adult, is in fact identical with his father (three-footed) ... and with his children (four-footed).

Oedipus has two sons, who communicate neither with him nor with each other; they kill each other. The myth, then, is an answer to the question how man can be the same, but different; how the rights and functions of king, father, husband, grandfather can remain the same while passing from one person to another; how the son can succeed the father without chaos ensuing.

Vernant now passes to the story about the Cypselids, tyrants of Corinth, that is recounted by Herodotus. Labda, the lame one, who belongs to the ruling clan of the Bacchiads, marries Eetion, a man of noble ancestry, but not highly regarded. An oracle tells Eetion that his son will be a rolling stone who will sweep away the rulers; Vernant thinks the point is that lame people have a rolling gait, but Cypselus came from a place called Petra (meaning rock), and a famous passage of Homer compares Hector rushing into battle at the head of his troops to a rolling stone fallen from a rock.[44] Men are sent to kill the infant Cypselus, but spare him, just as the shepherd spares the infant Oedipus; when they return to kill him, he has been hidden in a jar (*kypsele*). The jar, of course, gives the infant his name, but Vernant is reminded of the exposure of the infant Oedipus. Cypselus becomes tyrant and the father of the even greater tyrant Periander; Vernant notes a story told by Diogenes Laertius that Periander committed incest with his mother. He kills many of the men of Corinth, and to honour his wife Melissa, whom he has himself murdered, strips the women of their clothes, an act which Vernant holds to be equivalent to taking the women for himself. His son Lycophron refuses to speak to a father who has killed his mother, and goes off to Corcyra. Since he will not return while Periander is in Corinth, Periander plans to move to Corcyra, and the Corcyrians, not wishing to have a tyrant living among them, murder Lycophron.

This story seems to Vernant 'strangely parallel' to that of Oedipus.

> Tyranny springs from a disturbing marriage; lameness, oddness lead

[44] *Iliad*, 13.137.

> to tyranny; we find the sequence lameness-tyranny-power gained and lost, the continuous or clocked sequence of generations, straight or indirect succession, straightness or deviation in sexual relations, agreement or misunderstanding in a communication between fathers and sons, presence of mind or forgetfulness.

In the Greek imagination, Vernant concludes, the figure of the tyrant adopts the figure of the legendary hero. But is the parallel really so remarkable? It starts from the notion of lameness; Labda, like Labdacus, is lame. But as Rank notes in the work mentioned earlier, the hero in myths of this kind frequently springs from parents who are in some way disadvantaged, and the point of Labda's lameness surely is that she, like Eetion, falls within this category. Other features of each of the two stories recur in the history of many royal houses, in legend or in fact. A most suspicious feature of Vernant's version of the history of the house of Cadmus is the use he makes of the obscure story that the Sphinx was an illegitimate daughter of Laius, which is not attested before the second century A.D. and whose obvious Euhemerism indicates an origin not earlier than the Hellenistic Age. As for the tale of Periander's incest with his mother, Diogenes Laertius took it from the gossip-writer Aristippus, the most unreliable authority that can be imagined.[45]

I much admire the learning, ingenuity and courage of Jean-Pierre Vernant and sympathize with his impatience with the positivism of the interpretation of myth by scholars of the school of Nilsson. As he points out, one cannot help feeling that Greek myths must often have meant originally something very different from the meanings which they bore for the Greeks of historical times. But the attempt to recover these meanings is necessarily speculative; the danger of imposing structure, or better perhaps system, where there is none, or of imposing the wrong system, seems acute, and the Gallic neatness and tidiness of some of the structures contrasts disquietingly with the precariousness of the method by which they are obtained.[46] If one believes, as Lévi-Strauss believes and as Vernant seems to imply

[45] This was pointed out to me by Albert Henrichs.

[46] Vernant complains, *Myth and Society*, p.214, that in modern treatments of myth 'there is as yet no sign of the idea that religion and myth form an organized system whose coherence and complicated workings it is important to grasp'. There is some truth in this, but it is equally important to bear in mind that the 'system' came into existence in untidy and haphazard fashion.

that he does, that the structures one can discover in myths are based upon the logic of categories inherent in the mind, then one will be more optimistic about the prospects of success in such an operation than someone who like myself is unconvinced of this. English empiricists will watch the playing of this entertaining game with interest, and will scrutinize each separate claim according to the evidence; but they will long remain doubtful about the chances of building up a large body of results likely to command general assent.

We come now to the question of social psychology. One group of Freud's successors felt that he had considered the human being too much on his own and in isolation from the society and culture that surrounded him.[47] Anthropologists in field work became aware that what Freud had supposed to be features of the psychic make-up of every human being were often absent from some of the exotic cultures which they studied, and most found a notion of the collective unconscious to be unhelpful. European anthropologists, as Mr Huxley points out, were tolerant of diversity and so unwilling to accept Freud's unitary view of the human psyche; but American anthropologists, predisposed in his favour by their inheritance from the Enlightenment and by the need to mix all human types into the great melting-pot, showed more sympathy for Freud than did their European colleagues. In America Erich Fromm,[48] who had been connected with the Institut für Sozialforschung (Institute for Social Research) that had moved from Frankfurt to Columbia University in New York City, made a deep impression with his book *Escape from Freedom*, or *The Fear of Freedom* as it was called when published in Britain. In a deliberate effort to apply the methods of psychology to the problems of his time, Fromm used Marx as well as Freud. For him the key problem of psychology was that of the specific relation of the individual to the world; the psychological forces that had shaped history could be understood only if it was realized that they are socially conditioned. Fromm believed that the human individual had secured freedom from the traditional bonds of medieval society only to acquire together with his independence a new feeling of isolation and anxiety, so that he readily submitted to new kinds of compulsive

[47] For an account of this movement, see J.A.C. Brown, *Freud and the Post-Freudians* (Harmondsworth, 1961), pp.104f.

[48] On Fromm, see Brown, *Freud and the Post-Freudians*, pp.145f., and Leszek Kolakowski, *Main Currents of Marxism* (Oxford, 1978), 3.380f.

and irrational activity. Man could be liberated from this condition only by acquiring positive qualities which consisted in a spontaneous action of the total, integrated personality. The foremost component of such spontaneity was love 'as spontaneous affirmation of others, as the union of the individual with others on the basis of the preservation of the individual self'.[49] In obedience to Marxian theory Fromm argued that the dominant character traits of the regenerated society would in their turn become productive forms shaping the social process. At the end of his book, he demands a planned economy; there is almost as much of Christianity as of Marxism in his thinking, and he found a ready response among liberal supporters of the New Deal.

The social psychology of the new American school of anthropology on the one hand, and of neo-Freudians like Fromm and Abram Kardiner[50] on the other, were the main psychological influences on E.R. Dodds, when he wrote his famous book *The Greeks and the Irrational*, which, though ignored for some years after its publication in 1951, has enjoyed immense success, and has been beyond comparison the most influential application of post-Freudian psychology to the study of the ancient world.

In the first chapter Dodds discusses the apology that Agamemnon utters in the nineteenth book of the *Iliad*, when he has come to regret his rashness in provoking the quarrel with Achilles which has caused disaster. Agamemnon claims that he acted wrongly because cruel Ate, the goddess who takes away men's wits, was placed in his mind by Zeus and his portion, and the Erinys, the power that punishes men's crimes. This helps Agamemnon to save face, but it does not mean that he denies responsibility for his behaviour, for he pays over to Achilles the immense indemnity which he has promised him earlier. Dodds points out that not only wrong or foolish behaviour, but also sudden accesses of strength, exceptionally good ideas, or flashes of intelligence are often explained in Homer by the intervention of a deity, who, when it is impossible to identify him, is referred to as a *daimon*.

Wishing to find a psychological explanation for this mode of

[49] *The Fear of Freedom* (London, 1942), p.261. Anyone who wishes to understand the origins of Dodds, *The Greeks and the Irrational*, must read this book.

[50] Kardiner, *The Individual and his Society* (New York, 1939); *The Psychological Frontiers of Society* (New York, 1965).

thinking, Dodds points out that anthropology will not be slow to produce parallels, though he feels that these parallels will come from cultures too primitive to be quite respectable, and is surprised to find such an old-fashioned way of thinking in such a civilized and rational community as eighth-century Ionia. Rightly rejecting Nilsson's suggestion that Homeric heroes suffered from unusual mental instability, Dodds accounts for it in terms of two peculiarities which he thinks 'do unquestionably belong to the culture described by Homer'. The first of these is the alleged fact that Homer lacks a unified concept of the human personality, so that Homeric man lies open to external intervention; the second is the Greek habit of explaining what we call character or behaviour in terms of what a person knows.

The notion that Homer lacked a coherent concept of the self, first elucubrated by Hermann Fränkel and propagated by Bruno Snell, seems to be wholly false, and since I have lately restated my reasons for thinking so I will not repeat them now, being content to recall that when I first attacked the theory Devereux remarked to me with great truth that 'the moment a man says "I" this establishes at least a general sense of psychic coherence'.[51] In any case, if one believes in the possibility of divine monitions, one will scarcely suppose that a god cannot convey them unless the human mind happens to be specially 'open' in order to receive them. The second peculiarity means that when a man is faced with a decision that requires thought he will act upon his knowledge of what is right. Thus when in a famous passage in the eleventh book of the *Iliad* Odysseus is hard pressed in battle and must decide whether to fight or run away, he remembers the rule that cowards run away in battle, but brave men stand fast, and acts accordingly. Had Odysseus panicked and run, his failure to act on the knowledge which he undoubtedly possessed would have been set down to the action of a hostile deity. This, Dodds argues, would have enabled Odysseus to save face by projecting on to an external power his unbearable feelings of shame, and he suggests that it was because it enabled people to save face in such a manner that the primitive belief in divine motivation of certain human actions lingered on among the Greeks.

[51] See my *The Justice of Zeus*, 2nd edition (Berkeley and Los Angeles, 1983), which contains a new Epilogue, especially pp.9, 168, 188, 238.

I do not think that we need worry at finding Homer with his use of divine monitions in the less than respectable company of men belonging to primitive cultures like those found in Borneo and Ceylon; I have already quoted Kirk's remark that the first major development in the modern study of myth was the realization that the myths of primitive societies are highly relevant to the subject as a whole, and the same applies to the manner of conceiving mental happenings. Even later than Homer, Greek literature reveals many survivals from ancient times. But in any case the action attributed to the god never causes the human agent to deny responsibility; even when he is sure that a god has guided or misguided him, a man feels his action to have been his own. The belief explains how ideas, brilliant or disastrous, seem to come into our minds spontaneously, in a flash, without conscious reasoning, as though from an external source; and since it is not felt to abolish responsibility, it involves no real belief in a supernatural interference with the course of nature. After the fashion of such beliefs, it may well have lingered on in poetry long after it had ceased to play any significant part in ordinary thinking, all the more so because it had involved no real breach with realism or rationality.

Homeric man specially needed to get rid of his intolerable feelings of shame, Dodds argued, because the culture he belonged to was a shame-culture; but by the fifth century it had turned into a guilt-culture. These terms, coined, it would appear, by Erik Erikson, and taken by Dodds from Ruth Benedict, denote a classification of societies 'according to the predominance of one or another mechanism of social control, the mechanism by which people regulate their own conduct, and which others can invoke to punish conduct which transgresses the norm prevalent in a given society or a given period'.[52] The belief that Greek society changed from a shame-culture to a guilt-culture rests largely upon the comparison between two sorts of poetry: early epic, in which the notion of ritual pollution, associated with guilt feelings, is not prominent, and fifth-century tragedy, in which it is very prominent indeed. Dodds explained the change as being due to a sudden upsurge of feelings of guilt, caused by the loosening of family bonds, which made sons feel guilty because they came more and more into conflict with their

[52] See *The Justice of Zeus*, p.171, n.102.

fathers. But cultural changes of such magnitude do not often occur within so short a space of time in cultures at the kind of stage in their development which Greek culture had reached at the time in question; and in any case it is not easy to find instances of a culture in which both guilt and shame do not play some part. Far from having been new in the fifth century, belief in pollution must have been extremely ancient, and its lack of prominence in Homer may safely be set down, like the rarity of mention of Dionysus and Demeter, to the unwillingness of epic poetry to dwell on certain topics. The medical historian F. Kudlien[53] has argued that while the Greeks had a shame-culture they viewed disease either as a random evil or as a god's revenge for an offence against his honour; whereas while they had a guilt culture they viewed it as a punishment for wickedness. But Robert Parker[54] has shown that we find both attitudes during both periods, and they are not even inconsistent, since for a Greek what seemed like random evil could always be due to an offence committed by oneself or by some ancestor of which one was entirely unaware. 'The difference between "guilt-cultures" and "shame-cultures",' Sir Kenneth Dover writes,[55] 'seems to me a difference more in the way people talk than in the way they feel; if "guilt" means "fear of the gods" and "shame" "fear of the hostility and ridicule of other people", Greek culture contained both elements, and so does ours.'

In the fifth chapter of this book, Dodds put forward his theory that the notion of a soul separable from the body and able to leave it at intervals even during life was derived by the Greeks from Siberian shamanism. 'By crediting man with an occult self of divine origin,' he wrote, and thus setting body and soul at odds, the new religious pattern 'introduced into European culture a new interpretation of human existence, the interpretation we call puritanical.' Dodds argued that the doctrine of the rebirth of the soul, which as a corollary of this was propagated by those holding the beliefs called Orphic or Pythagorean, was a response to 'a deeper psychological need – the need to rationalise these unexplained feelings of guilt

[53] 'Early Greek primitive medicine', in *Clio Medica*, 3 (1968).

[54] *Miasma: Pollution and Purification in Early Greek Religion* (Oxford, 1983), p.251 with n.90.

[55] *Greek Popular Morality in the Time of Plato and Aristotle* (Oxford, 1974), p.220, n.3.

which, as we saw earlier, were prevalent during the Archaic Age'. 'Men were conscious,' he continued,

> and on Freud's view, rightly conscious – that such feelings had their roots in a submerged and long-forgotten past experience. What more natural than to interpret that intuition (which is in fact, according to Freud, a faint awareness of infantile traumata) as a faint awareness of sin committed in a former life?[56]

Dodds's theory, first put forward by Karl Meuli, that the belief that the soul could quit the body derived ultimately from Central Asia, is by no means certain to be right; J.N. Bremmer[57] has now shown, using much comparative material from Indian and other Indo-European sources, that the Greeks possessed from early times the belief in a separable soul, the *psyche*, which survived the body and was distinct from the seat of the intelligence, denoted by such terms as *nous* and *thymos*. Belief in metempsychosis, held by Pythagoras during the sixth century B.C., may have come from Asia, though India by way of Egypt seems to me a possible alternative. But here I am most concerned to draw attention to the speculative nature of Dodds's explanation of the rebirth of the soul; why should the fear of divine justice be equated with the guilt feelings engendered by Oedipal memories of the kind which Freudian theory postulated?

Dodds holds that what he called the Enlightenment of the sixth and fifth centuries B.C. stimulated a violent reaction, finding expression first in the prosecution of distinguished thinkers for impiety, but affecting the social fabric in a more permanent way by means of a recrudescence of various superstitions. But the so-called Enlightenment – the very use of the term is calculated to suggest misleading analogies – affected ordinary people far less than this argument assumed. Much of the evidence alleged to attest the persecution of intellectuals is most uncertain, as Dover has shown in a brief but important article,[58] and popular superstition can hardly have become intensified after the fifth century, though no doubt it became more articulate, because it had never ceased to be intense.

Dodds, as I have mentioned, showed that Plato and Aristotle,

[56] *The Greeks and the Irrational*, pp.139, 151-2.
[57] *The Ancient Greek Concept of the Soul* (Princeton, 1983).
[58] *Talenta*, 7 (1976); cf. *The Justice of Zeus*, pp.230f. with the additional note on p.248.

while rational in a high degree themselves, were fully aware of the need to study the irrational elements in human behaviour; but he criticizes Hellenistic philosophers, and particularly the Stoics, for going back behind Plato and Aristotle to the naive intellectualism of the fifth century. In speaking of the rapid decline of Greek culture, which set in from about the beginning of the second century B.C., Dodds compares the new anti-intellectualism of that time with the Romantic reaction against the rationalistic natural theology of the eighteenth century. When he comes to the problem of how we are to account for that decline, Dodds invokes 'the fear of freedom – the unconscious flight from the heavy burden of choice which an open society lays upon its members'. 'For the refusal of responsibility in any sphere,' he continues, 'there is always a price to be paid, usually in the form of neurosis'; the influence of Fromm is unmistakable. Dodds illustrates this by reference to some of the more striking examples of religious neurosis and superstitious eccentricity of the kind he was to deal with later, in his study of the imperial period. Dodds admits that at this point in the enquiry he has his own time in mind, and allows himself to express a guarded optimism. The ancients, he writes, had no instrument for understanding [the Irrational], still less for controlling it; and in the Hellenistic Age too many of them made the mistake of thinking that they could ignore it. Modern man, on the other hand, is beginning to acquire such an instrument. It is still very far from perfect, Dodds went on,

> nor is it always skilfully handled; in many fields, including that of history, its possibilities still have to be tested. Yet it seems to offer the hope that if we use it wisely we shall eventually understand our horse better; that, understanding him better, we shall be able by better training to overcome his fears; and that through the overcoming of fear horse and rider will one day take that decisive jump, and take it successfully.[59]

Fromm, it will be remembered, had hoped that freedom might be attained 'by means of the spontaneous action of the integrated personality'. In the year before Dodds's book was published, Melanie Klein had expressed the hope that psychoanalysis might go beyond

[59] *The Greeks and the Irrational*, pp.252, 254-5.

the single individual in its range of operation and influence the life of mankind as a whole. 'We are ready to believe,' she continued,

> that what would now seem a Utopian state of things may well come true in those distant days when, as I hope, child analysis will become as much a part of every person's upbringing as school-education is now. Then perhaps that hostile attitude, springing from fear and suspicion, which is latent more or less strongly in every human being, and which intensifies a hundredfold in him each impulse of destruction, will give way to kindlier and more trustful feelings towards his fellow men, and people may inhabit the earth together in greater peace and goodwill than they do now.[60]

Such was the optimism of that post-war decade when in their different ways Wilhelm Reich, Herbert Marcuse and Norman O. Brown all proclaimed their confidence that one day repression would be abolished and a Freudo-Marxian Utopia realized. Freud himself had been less optimistic; and in our time, even in New York, where the well-to-do may enjoy for a consideration, which makes it still more valuable, the luxury of the confessional in an up-to-date package administered by that new analyst who is but old priest writ large, such simple faith is not often encountered. Dodds's splendid book, fully documented, elegantly written, and giving a detailed account of many concrete phenomena, will still be useful many years from now. The parts of it that are already showing signs of wear are just those parts in which the influence of psychoanalysis and of the social anthropology that sprang from it is most perceptible. After considering his work, one can hardly bear to turn to other attempts to apply social psychology to the study of antiquity.

All this applies still more to Dodds's later work, *Pagan and Christian in an Age of Anxiety*. He finds that 'contempt for the human condition and hatred of the body was a disease endemic in the entire culture of the period' between the time of Marcus Aurelius and that of Constantine, a state of affairs which he attributes to 'an endogenous neurosis, an index of intense and wide-spread guilt-feeling'. What the Gnostic writer Valentinus called *Bythos*, he says, 'the mysterious primordial Deep where all things originally dwelt unknown,

[60] Cited from Anthony Storr, *Human Aggression* (London, 1968), pp.2-3.

corresponds to what Augustine called the *abyssus humanae conscientiae*, and to what we call the Unconscious'; in his view the Gnostic and the Manichean splitting of God into a good god and a bad god 'seems to reflect a splitting of the individual father-image into its corresponding emotional components'.[61] The second chapter, 'Man and the daemonic world', devotes much space to sketches of the pathological peculiarities of Aelius Aristides, of Peregrinus, the religious charlatan described by Lucian in a comic account which Dodds strangely takes as factual narrative,[62] and of the Christian martyr St Perpetua;[63] it is a little as if the author of a study of the intellectual climate of Victorian England were to devote a corresponding proportion of his limited space to the spiritual biographies of John Ruskin, Lewis Carroll, and Helena Petrovna-Blavatsky. The 'age of anxiety' is an illusion, or at least a very partial view, created by the selective use of evidence; the religions and philosophies which Dodds describes certainly took a low view of this world in comparison with the divine world, but most of them were concerned to offer ways of compensating for this disadvantage by establishing some kind of communication with the higher powers. Ramsay MacMullen[64] has lately protested against the excessive attention paid by some scholars, among whom Dodds must certainly be numbered, to Gnostic Hermetic, Chaldaean, Orphic or Neoplatonic texts and against the neglect of the evidence furnished by papyri and inscriptions in the attempt to put together a general picture of the religion of the age. Walter Burkert, in the Jackson Lectures on the mystery religions which I was fortunate enough to hear him deliver at Harvard in 1982, differed markedly from earlier interpreters, such as Cumont and Reitzenstein, in according comparatively little prominence to the other-worldly aspects and the

[61] *Pagan and Christian in an Age of Anxiety*, pp.35-6, 19-20.

[62] In the same way Dodds draws an inference about the Greek attitude to the gods in the Hellenistic period which I would hesitate to accept by taking wholly seriously the paean of Hermocles in honour of Demetrius Poliorcetes. See J.U. Powell, *Collectanea Alexandrina* (Oxford, 1925), p.173. At the right time and place, the Greek gods, unlike most others, could take a joke; see *The Justice of Zeus*, pp.210f. with n.24. On Dodds's treatment of Peregrinus, see D.A. Russell, *Proceedings of the British Academy*, 67 (1981).

[63] For an attractive Freudian suggestion about this saint see Lefkowitz, *Heroines and Hysterics*, pp.53f.

[64] *Paganism in the Roman Empire* (New Haven and London, 1981), especially pp.62f.

Oriental elements of these cults, and in showing that while they might hope to improve the position of their members in the next world, they did not promise them eternal life, but were most of all concerned to improve their position in this world, by winning them the protection of a higher power. I am not persuaded that the adherents of these and the numerous other religions and philosophies of the time would have been greatly better off had there been added to the many and often bizarre would-be saviours competing for their attention the ambiguous figure of the Freudian analyst.[65]

[65] In comparison with that of Dodds, most attempts to apply social psychology to the study of the ancient world are of slight importance. Devereux's valuable article 'Greek pseudo-homosexuality and the "Greek miracle" ', *Symbolae Osloenses*, 42 (1967), owes its strength to its sociological component, not to any element that derives from psychoanalysis.

I am grateful to Ruth Padel, Albert Henrichs and Robert Parker for helpful criticisms.

Select Bibliography

Barzun, Jacques, *Clio and the Doctors* (Chicago and London, 1974)

Bettelheim, Bruno, *Freud and Man's Soul* (New York, 1983)

Bonaparte, Marie, Anna Freud and Ernst Kris (eds), *The Origins of Psycho-Analysis* (London, 1954)

Brown, J.A.C., *Freud and the Post-Freudians* (London, 1961)

Clark, Ronald W., *Freud: The Man and the Cause* (London, 1982)

Davis, Robert Con (ed.), *The Fictional Father: Lacanian Readings of the Text* (Amherst, Mass., 1981)

Dewhurst, Kenneth, and Nigel Reeves, *Friedrich Schiller: Medicine, Psychology and Literature* (Oxford, 1978)

Dodds, E.R., *The Greeks and the Irrational* (Berkeley and Los Angeles, 1951)

—, *Pagan and Christian in an Age of Anxiety* (Cambridge, 1965)

Ellenberger, Henri F., *The Discovery of the Unconscious: The History and Evolution of Dynamic Psychiatry* (London, 1970)

Farrell, B.A., *The Standing of Psychoanalysis* (Oxford, 1981)

Freud, Sigmund, *Letters of Sigmund Freud, 1873-1939*, translated by Tania and James Stern (London, 1961)

Gabriel, Yannis, *Freud and Society* (London, 1983)

Gay, Peter, *Freud, Jews and Other Germans* (Oxford, 1979)

Jacoby, Russell, *Social Amnesia: A Critique of Contemporary Psychology from Adler to Laing* (Boston, 1975)

Jones, Ernest, *Sigmund Freud: Life and Work*, 3 vols (London, 1953-7)

Kirk, G.S., *Myth: Its Meaning and Functions in Ancient and Other Cultures* (Cambridge, 1970)

Kris, Ernst, *Psychoanalytic Explorations in Art* (New York, 1952)

Lacan, Jacques, *Ecrits: A Selection* (London, 1977)

Lloyd-Jones, Hugh, *The Justice of Zeus*, 2nd edition (Berkeley and

Los Angeles, 1983)

Ricoeur, Paul, *Freud and Philosophy: An Essay on Interpretation* (New Haven, Conn., 1977).

Rieff, Philip, *Freud: The Mind of the Moralist*, 3rd edition (Chicago and London, 1979)

Róheim, Géza, *Psychoanalysis and Anthropology* (New York, 1950)

Rycroft, Charles, *A Critical Dictionary of Psychoanalysis* (London, 1968)

—, *The Innocence of Dreams* (London, 1979)

Sartre, Jean-Paul, *L'idiot de la famille*, 3 vols (Paris, 1971-2)

Spector, Jack J., *The Aesthetics of Freud* (London, 1972)

Spindler, G.D. (ed.), *The Making of Psychological Anthropology* (Berkeley and Los Angeles, 1978)

Stannard, David E., *Shrinking History: On Freud and the Failure of Psychohistory* (New York and Oxford, 1980)

Sulloway, Frank J., *Freud: Biologist of the Mind* (London, 1979)

Timpanaro, Sebastiano, *The Freudian Slip* (London, 1976)

Turkle, Sherry, *Psychoanalytic Politics: Jacques Lacan and Freud's French Revolution* (London, 1979)

Vernant, Jean-Pierre, *Tragedy and Myth in Ancient Greece* (Brighton, 1981)

Weber, Samuel, *The Legend of Freud* (Minneapolis, 1982)

Wilkinson, Elizabeth M., *Schiller, Poet or Philosopher?* (Oxford, 1961)

Wollheim, Richard, *Freud*, Modern Masters (London, 1971)

— and James Hopkins (eds), *Philosophical Essays on Freud* (Cambridge, 1982)

Index

psa. = psychoanalysis